THE
TREATY OF WASHINGTON:

ITS

NEGOTIATION, EXECUTION,

AND THE DISCUSSIONS RELATING THERETO.

BY

CALEB CUSHING.

BOOKS FOR LIBRARIES PRESS
FREEPORT, NEW YORK

First Published 1873
Reprinted 1970

STANDARD BOOK NUMBER:
8369-5277-4

LIBRARY OF CONGRESS CATALOG CARD NUMBER:
72-114872

PRINTED IN THE UNITED STATES OF AMERICA

INSCRIBED,

IN TESTIMONY OF PROFOUND RESPECT,

TO

COUNT FREDERIC SCLOPIS, OF SALERANO,

MINISTER OF STATE,

SENATOR OF THE KINGDOM OF ITALY.

CONTENTS.

	PAGE
CHAPTER I. *INTRODUCTION*	9
CHAPTER II. *ALABAMA CLAIMS*	15
Conduct of Great Britain toward the United States during the late Civil War	15
Negotiations by Mr. Seward	17
Policy of President Grant	18
Overtures by Great Britain	20
Stipulations respecting the *Alabama* Claims	21
Arrangements of Arbitration	26
The American Case	30
Explanation of Objections to the American Case	33
Agitation respecting the National Claims	34
Cause of this Agitation	39
Discussion between the two Governments	42
English Misconception of American Sentiment	48
Attitude of the American Government	52
Action of the American Agent and Counsel	55
Presentation of Counter-Cases	57

CONTENTS.

	PAGE
Negotiations for a Supplemental Treaty	62
Presentation of Arguments for the United States	66
Decision of the Arbitrators respecting National Losses	69
Seat of the Arbitration	74
Count Frederic Sclopis	77
Mr. Stæmpfli	80
Viscount of Itajubá	84
Sir Alexander Cockburn	86
Mr. Charles Francis Adams	93
Secretary of the Tribunal	94
Agents and Counsel	94
Efforts of the British Government to obtain Reargument	99
Rules concerning the Conferences of the Tribunal	106
Discussions of the Tribunal	109
Sir Alexander Cockburn's Call for Reargument	111
Case of the *Florida* decided	114
Special Arguments ordered on Certain Points	117
Case of the *Alabama* decided	118
Case of the *Shenandoah* decided	120
The Special Arguments	121
Question of Damages	124
Final Judgment of the Tribunal	125
Announcement of the Decision	126
Conduct of the British Arbitrator	128

CONTENTS.

	PAGE
Sir Alexander Cockburn's Reasons for Dissent	128
Review of Sir Alexander Cockburn's "Reasons"	130
Opinions of the other Arbitrators	149
Review of the Decision of the Tribunal on National Losses	153
Decision as to Private Losses	159
Effect of the Award	164
Validity of the Award	167
Filibuster Objections	177
Sale of Arms not affected by the Treaty or the Award	180
Question of Supplies of Coal	180
What the United States have gained by the Award	184

CHAPTER III. *MISCELLANEOUS CLAIMS* 187

Treaty Provisions	187
Private Claims on Governments	189
Usefulness of Mixed Commissions	193
Other Forms of Arbitration	195
Tendency of Reason and Justice to prevail over Force	197
Theory of Arbitration	200
Wisdom of the present Mixed Commission	201

CHAPTER IV. *THE NORTHWESTERN BOUNDARY-LINE* .. 203

Provisions of the Treaty	203
History of the Question	205
The Award	221

CONTENTS.

	PAGE
CHAPTER V. *THE FISHERIES*	226
History of the Question	226
Provisions of the Treaty of Washington	237
Probable Amount of Indemnity	239
CHAPTER VI. *COMMERCIAL INTERCOURSE AND TRANSPORTATION*	241
Treaty Provisions	241
Relation of the British Provinces to the United States	247
APPENDIX.—*THE TREATY OF WASHINGTON*	257
THE DECISION AND AWARD	275

THE TREATY OF WASHINGTON.

CHAPTER I.

INTRODUCTION.

The Treaty of Washington, whether it be regarded in the light of its general spirit and object, of its particular stipulations, or of its relation to the high contracting parties, constitutes one of the most notable and interesting of all the great diplomatic acts of the present age.

It disposes, in forty-three articles, of five different subjects of controversy between Great Britain and the United States, two of them European or imperial, three American or colonial, and some of them of such nature as most imminently to imperil the precious peace of the two great English-speaking nations.

Indeed, several of these objects of controversy are questions coeval with the national existence of the United States, and which, if lost sight of occasionally in the midst of other pre-occupations of peace or war, yet continually came to the surface again from time to time to vex and disturb the good understanding of both Governments. Others of the questions, although of more modern date, incidents of our late Civil War, were all the more irritating, as being fresh wounds to the sensibility of the people of the United States.

If, to all these considerations, be added the fact that negotiation after negotiation respecting these questions had failed to resolve them in a satisfactory manner, it will be readily seen how great was the diplomatic triumph achieved by the Treaty of Washington.

It required peculiar inducements and agencies to accomplish this great result.

Prominent among the inducements were the pacific spirit of the President of the United States and the Queen of Great Britain, and of their respective Cabinets, and the sincere and heartfelt desire of a great majority of the people of both countries that no shadow of offense should be allowed any longer to linger on the face of their international relations.

Great Britain, it is but just to her to say, if not confessedly conscious of wrong, yet, as being the party to whom wrong was imputed, did honorably and wisely make the decisive advance toward reconciliation, by consenting to dispatch five Commissioners to Washington, there, under the eye of the President, to treat with five Commissioners on behalf of the United States.

Diplomatic congresses have assembled on previous occasions to terminate the great wars of Europe, or to maintain and consolidate peace in America. And conferences, like those of Vienna, of Aix-la-Chapelle, of Paris, may have embraced the representation and settled the interests of a larger number of nations; but they did not consist of higher personages, nor did they treat of larger matters than did the conference of Washington.

On the part of the United States were five persons, —Hamilton Fish, Robert C. Schenck, Samuel Nelson, Ebenezer Rockwood Hoar, and George H. Williams,—eminently fit representatives of the diplomacy, the bench, the bar, and the legislature of the United States: on the part of Great Britain, Earl De Grey and Ripon, President of the Queen's Council; Sir Stafford Northcote, ex-Minister and actual Member of the House of Commons; Sir Edward Thornton, the universally respected British Minister at Washington; Sir John Macdonald, the able and eloquent Premier of the Canadian Dominion; and, in revival of the good old time, when learning was equal to any other title of public honor, the Universities in the person of Professor Mountague Bernard.

With persons of such distinction and character, it was morally impossible that the negotiation should fail: the negotiators were *bound* to succeed. Their reputations, not less than the honor of their respective countries, were at stake. The circumstances involved moral coercion, more potent than physical force. The issues of peace and of war were in the hands of those ten personages. They were to illustrate the eternal truth that, out of the differences of nations, competent statesmen evolve peace; and that it is only by the incompetency of statesmen of one side or the other,—that is, their ignorance, their passion, their prejudice, their want of forecast, or their willfully aggressive ambition,—that the unspeakable calamities of war are ever thrust on the suffering world. Neither Mr. Fish nor Earl De Grey, nor their respective associates, could afford to take on their consciences the responsibility, or on their characters the shame, of the nonsuccess on this occasion of a last effort to renovate and re-establish in perpetuity relations of cordial friendship between Great Britain and the United States. And, if they needed other impulse to right conclusion, that was given by the wise and firm direction of the President, here in person, and of the Queen, here in effect through the means of daily telegraphic communication.

Happily for the peace of the two countries and for the welfare of the world, the negotiators proved equal to the emergency, in courage as well as in statesmanship. The Government and the people of Great Britain had learned to regret sincerely the occurrence of the acts or facts which had given such deep offense, and which had done such serious injury, to the United States; and, moreover, the Government and people of this country had come to desire, with equal sincerity, that some honorable solution of the existing difficulties might be found, so as to leave room for the unobstructed action here of the prevailing natural tendency toward unreserved intellectual and commercial association with Great Britain. Material interests,

INTRODUCTION. 13

social sentiments, incidental circumstances, all invited both nations to cordial reunion.

In the face of many difficulties, the Commissioners, on the 8th of May, 1871, completed a treaty, which received the prompt approval of their respective Governments; which has passed unscathed through the severest ordeal of a temporary misunderstanding between the two Governments respecting the construction of some of its provisions; which has already attained the dignity of a monumental act in the estimation of mankind; and which is destined to occupy hereafter a lofty place in the history of the diplomacy and the international jurisprudence of Europe and America.

Coming now to the analysis of this treaty, we find that Articles I. to XI. inclusive make provisions for the settlement by arbitration of the injuries alleged to have been suffered by the United States in consequence of the fitting out, arming, or equipping, in the ports of Great Britain, of Confederate cruisers to make war on the United States.

Articles XII. to XVII. inclusive make provision to settle, by means of a mixed Commission, all claims on either side for injuries by either Government to the citizens of the other during the late Civil War, other than claims growing out of the acts of Confederate cruisers disposed of by the previous articles of the Treaty.

Articles XVIII. to XXV. inclusive contain provisions for the permanent regulation of the coast fisheries on the Atlantic shores of the United States and of the British Provinces of Quebec, Nova Scotia, and

New Brunswick, and the Colony of Prince Edward's Island [including the Colony of Newfoundland by Article XXXII.].

Articles XXVI. to XXXIII. inclusive provide for the reciprocal free navigation of certain rivers, including the River St. Lawrence; for the common use of certain canals in the Canadian Dominion and in the United States; for the free navigation of Lake Michigan; for reciprocal free transit across the territory either of the United States or of the Canadian Dominion, as the case may be: the whole, subject to legislative provisions hereafter to be enacted by the several Governments.

Articles XXXIV. to XLII. provide for determining by arbitration which of two different channels between Vancouver's Island and the main-land constitutes the true boundary-line in that region of the territories of the United States and Great Britain.

Each of these five distinct classes of questions will receive separate consideration.

CHAPTER II.

ALABAMA CLAIMS.

CONDUCT OF GREAT BRITAIN TOWARD THE UNITED STATES DURING THE LATE CIVIL WAR.

AT the conclusion of the Civil War, intense feeling of indignation against Great Britain pervaded the minds of the Government and Congress of the United States, and of the people of those of the States which had devoted themselves to maintaining in arms the integrity of the Union against the hostile efforts of the Southern Confederation.

We charged and we believed that Great Britain and her Colonies had been the arsenal, the navy-yard, and the treasury of the Confederates.

We charged and we believed that Confederate cruisers, which had depredated largely on our shipping and maritime commerce, never could have taken and never held the sea, but for the partiality and gross negligence of the British Government.

We charged and we believed that but for the premature recognition of the belligerence of the Confederates by Great Britain, and the direct aid or supplies which were subsequently furnished to them in British ports, the insurrection in the Southern States never would have assumed, or could not have retained, those gigantic proportions, which served to render it so costly of blood and of treasure to the whole Union, and so specially disastrous to the Southern States themselves.

We charged and we believed that, in all this, Great Britain, through her Government, had disregarded the obligations of neutrality imposed on her by the law of nations to such manifest degree as to have afforded to the United States just and ample cause of war.

The United States, through all these events, with William H. Seward, as Secretary of State, and Charles Francis Adams, Minister at London, had not failed to address continual remonstrances to the British Government, demanding reparation for past wrong and the cessation from continuous wrong: which remonstrances did, in fact, at length awaken the British Government to greater vigilance in the discharge of its international duties, but could not induce it to take any step toward reparation so long as Earl Russell [then Lord John Russell], by whose negligence or misjudgment the injuries had happened, remained in charge of the foreign affairs of the Government. That statesman, while, on more than one occasion, expressly admitting the wrong done to the United States, still persisted, with singular obtuseness or narrowness of mind, in maintaining that the *honor* of England would not permit her to make any reparation to the United States.

Never, in the history of nations, has an occasion existed where a powerful people, smarting under the consciousness of injury, manifested greater magnanimity than was displayed in that emergency by the United States.

We had on the sea hundreds of ships of war or of transport; we had on land hundreds of thousands of veteran soldiers under arms; we had officers of land and sea, the combatants in a hundred battles: all this vast force of war was in a condition to be launched as a thunderbolt at any enemy; and, in the present case, the possessions of that enemy, whether continental or insular, lay at our very door in tempting helplessness.

But neither the Government and people of the United States, nay, nor their laurel-crowned Generals and Admirals, desired war as a choice, nor would accept it but as a necessity; and they elected to continue to negotiate with Great Britain, and to do what no great European State has ever done under like circumstances,—that is, to disarm absolutely, and make thorough trial of the experiment of generous forbearance before having recourse to the dread extremity of vengeful hostilities against Great Britain.

NEGOTIATIONS BY MR. SEWARD.

The event justified our conduct. To the prejudiced and impracticable Lord Russell, there succeeded in charge of the foreign affairs of the British Government, first, Lord Stanley [now the Earl of Derby], and then the Earl of Clarendon, who, more wise and just than he, successively entered upon negotiations with the United States on that very basis of arbitration which he had so peremptorily rejected, but which Mr. Seward persisted in asserting as wise in itself and honorable to both Governments.

Those negotiations failed. But the rejection by the Senate of the Clarendon-Johnson Treaty, with Mr. Sumner's commentary thereon, if it had the apparent effect, at first, of widening the breach between the two countries by the irritation it produced in England, yet ultimately had the opposite effect by forcing on public attention there a more general and clearer perception of the wrong which had been done to the United States.

POLICY OF PRESIDENT GRANT.

At this stage of the question, President Grant came into office; and he and his advisers seem to have well judged that it sufficed for him, after giving expression fully and distinctly to his own view of the questions at issue, there to pause and wait for the tranquillization of opinion in England, and the probable initiation of new negotiations by the British Government.

It happened as the President anticipated, and with attendant circumstances of peculiar interest to the United States.

During the late war between Germany and France, the condition of Europe was such as to induce the British Ministers to take into consideration the foreign relations of Great Britain; and, as Lord Granville, the British Minister of Foreign Affairs, has himself stated in the House of Lords, they saw cause to look with solicitude on the uneasy relations of the British Government with the United States, and the inconvenience thereof in case of possible complications in Europe. Thus impelled, the Government dispatched to Washington a gentleman, who enjoyed the confidence of both Cabinets, Sir John Rose, to ascertain whether overtures for re-opening negotiations would be received by the President in spirit and terms acceptable to Great Britain.

It was the second time, in the present generation, that the foreign policy of England had been directed by a sense of the importance to her of maintaining good relations with the United States; for, by arguing from that point, France, at the opening of war with Prussia, induced the British Government to desist from those excessive belligerent pretensions to the prejudice of neutrals, which in former times had served to embroil her with both France and the United States.

There is another fact, which, in my opinion, powerfully contributed to induce this overture on the part of the British Government, although it was not spoken of in this connection by Lord Granville. I allude to the President's recommendation to Congress to appoint a commission to audit the claims of American citizens on Great Britain growing out of the acts of Confederate cruisers, in view of having them assumed by the Government of the United States. In this incident there was matter of grave and serious reflection to Great Britain.

On arriving at Washington, Sir John Rose found

the United States disposed to meet with perfect correspondence of good-will the advances of the British Government.

OVERTURES BY GREAT BRITAIN.

Accordingly, on the 26th of January, 1871, the British Government, through Sir Edward Thornton, formally proposed to the American Government the appointment of a joint High Commission to hold its sessions at Washington, and there devise means to settle the various pending questions between the two Governments affecting the British possessions in North America.

To this overture Mr. Fish replied that the President would with pleasure appoint, as invited, Commissioners on the part of the United States, provided the deliberations of the Commissioners should be extended to other differences,—that is to say, to include the differences growing out of incidents of the late Civil War: without which, in his opinion, the proposed Commission would fail to establish those permanent relations of sincere and substantial friendship between the two countries which he, in common with the Queen, desired to have prevail.

The British Government promptly accepted this proposal for enlarging the sphere of the negotiation, with the result, as we have already seen, of the conclusion of the Treaty of Washington.

STIPULATIONS RESPECTING THE ALABAMA CLAIMS.

The Treaty begins by describing the differences, which we are now considering, as differences " growing out of the acts committed by the several vessels, which have given rise to the claims generically known as the *Alabama Claims;*" which are further described as " all the said claims growing out of acts committed by the aforesaid vessels, and generically known as the *Alabama Claims.*"

Note that the subject of difference is stated in terms of absolute, although specific, universality, as *all* the claims on the part of the United States growing out of the acts of certain vessels. No exception is made of any particular claims growing out of those acts. And reference is not made to *certain* admitted claims by the British Government: on the contrary, it is expressly declared in the Treaty that the " complaints" and " claims" of the United States, without any discrimination between them, " are not admitted by the British Government."

At the same time, the British Commissioners, by authority of the Queen, express, " in a friendly spirit, the regret felt by Her Majesty's Government for the escape, under whatever circumstances, of the *Alabama* and other vessels from British ports, and for the depredations committed by those vessels."

Whereupon, " in order to remove and adjust all complaints and claims on the part of the United States, and to provide for the speedy settlement of such claims," the contracting parties agree that all the said claims, growing out of acts committed by the aforesaid vessels, and generically known as the *Alabama* Claims, shall be referred to a Tribunal of Arbitration to be composed of five Arbitrators, appointed in the following manner,—namely, one by the President of the United States, and one by the Queen of the United Kingdom, with request to the King of Italy, the President of the Swiss Confederation, and the Emperor of Brazil, each to name an Arbitrator; and, on the omission of either of those personages to act, then with a like request to the King of Sweden and Norway.

The Treaty further provides that the Arbitrators shall meet at Geneva, in Switzerland, at the earliest convenient day after they shall have been named, and shall proceed impartially and carefully to examine and decide all questions which shall be laid before them on the part of either Government.

In deciding the matters submitted to the Arbitrators, it is provided that they shall be governed by certain rules, which are agreed upon by the parties as rules to be taken as applicable to the case, and by such principles of international law, not inconsistent therewith, as the Arbitrators shall determine to have been applicable to the case, which rules are as follows:

"A neutral Government is bound—

"First, to use due diligence to prevent the fitting out, arming, or equipping, within its jurisdiction, of any vessel which it has reasonable ground to believe is intended to cruise or to carry on war against a Power with which it is at peace; and also to use like diligence to prevent the departure from its jurisdiction of any vessel intended to cruise or carry on war as above, such vessel having been specially adapted, in whole or in part, within such jurisdiction, to warlike use.

"Secondly, not to permit or suffer either belligerent to make use of its ports or waters as the base of naval operations against the other, or for the purpose of the renewal or augmentation of military supplies or arms, or the recruitment of men.

"Thirdly, to exercise due diligence in its own ports and waters, and, as to all persons within its jurisdiction, to prevent any violation of the foregoing obligations and duties."

Great Britain, it is added in the Treaty by way of explanation, can not assent to the foregoing rules as a statement of principles of international law which were actually in force at the time when the claims in question arose; but, in order to evince her desire of strengthening the friendly relations between the two countries, and of making satisfactory provision for the future, she agrees that, in deciding the questions arising out of such claims, the Arbitrators should assume that she had undertaken to act upon the principles set forth in these rules.

And the Parties proceed to stipulate to observe these rules as between themselves in the future, and to bring them to the knowledge of other maritime Powers, and to invite the latter to accede thereto.

In respect of procedure, the Treaty provides that each of the two Parties shall name one person to attend the Tribunal as its agent or representative; that the written or printed case of each of the two Parties, accompanied by the documents, the official correspondence, and other evidence on which each relies, shall be delivered in duplicate to each of the

Arbitrators and to the agent of the other Party, as soon as may be after the organization of the Tribunal; that within four months after the delivery on both sides of the written or printed case, either Party may, in like manner, deliver in duplicate to each of the said Arbitrators and to the agent of the other Party a counter-case, and additional documents, correspondence, and evidence, in reply to the case, documents, correspondence, and evidence so presented by the other Party; that it shall be the duty of the agent of each Party, within two months after the expiration of the time limited for the delivery of the counter-case on both sides, to deliver in duplicate to each of the said Arbitrators and to the agent of the other Party a written or printed argument showing the points and referring to the evidence upon which his Government relies.

No express provision for the appointment of counsel appears in the Treaty; but they are recognized in the clause which declares that the Arbitrators may, if they desire further elucidation with regard to any point, require a written or printed statement or argument, or oral argument, by counsel upon it; but in such case the other Party shall be entitled to reply either orally or in writing, as the case may be.

Finally, with reference to procedure, it is stipulated that the Tribunal shall first determine as to each vessel separately, whether Great Britain has, by any act or omission, failed to fulfill any of the duties set forth in the Treaty rules, or recognized by the principles of international law not inconsistent with such rules, and shall certify such fact as to each of the said vessels. This decision shall, if possible, be reached within three months from the close of the argument on both sides.

In case the Tribunal finds that Great Britain has failed to fulfill any duty or duties as aforesaid, it may, if it think proper, proceed to award a sum in gross to be paid by Great Britain to the United States for all the claims referred to it; and in such case the gross sum so awarded shall be paid in coin by the Government of Great Britain to the Government of the United States, at Washington, within twelve months after the date of the award.

In case the Tribunal finds that Great Britain has failed to fulfill any duty or duties as aforesaid, and does not award a sum in gross, the Parties agree that a Board of Assessors shall be appointed to ascertain and determine what claims are valid, and what amount or amounts shall be paid by Great Britain to the United States on account of the liability arising from such failure, as to each vessel, according to the extent of such liability as decided by the Arbitrators. This Board to be constituted as follows: One member thereof to be named by the United States, one by Great Britain, and one by the Representative at Washington of the King of Italy.

In conclusion, the Parties engage to consider the result of the proceedings of the Tribunal of Arbitration and of the Board of Assessors, should such Board be appointed, " as a full, perfect, and final settlement of all the claims" in question; and further engage that "every such claim, whether the same may or may not have been presented to the notice of, made, preferred, or laid before the Tribunal or Board, shall, from and after the conclusion of the proceedings of the Tribunal or Board, be considered and treated as finally settled, barred, and thenceforth inadmissible."

ARRANGEMENTS OF ARBITRATION.

The appointment of Arbitrators took place in due course, and with the ready good-will of the three neutral Governments. The United States appointed Mr. Charles Francis Adams; Great Britain appointed Sir Alexander Cockburn; the King of Italy named Count Frederic Sclopis; the President of the Swiss Confederation, Mr. Jacob Stæmpfli; and the Emperor of Brazil, the Baron d'Itajubá.

Mr. J. C. Bancroft Davis was appointed Agent of the United States, and Lord Tenterden of Great Britain.

The Tribunal was organized for the reception of the case of each Party, and held its first conference on the 15th of December, 1871.

On the motion of Mr. Adams, seconded by Sir Alexander Cockburn, it was voted that Count Sclopis, as being the Arbitrator named by the first Power mentioned in the Treaty after Great Britain and the United States, should preside over the labors of the Tribunal.

I observe in passing, as will be more distinctly seen

hereafter, that the personal fitness of Count Sclopis also rendered it eminently proper that he should preside; for he was the senior in age of all the Arbitrators, of exalted social condition, and distinguished as a man of letters, a jurist, and a statesman.

On the proposal of Count Sclopis, the Tribunal of Arbitration requested the Arbitrator named by the President of the Swiss Confederation to recommend some suitable person to act as the Secretary of the Tribunal. Mr. Stæmpfli named for this office Mr. Alexandre Favrot, and he was accordingly appointed Secretary.

The printed Case of the United States, with accompanying documents, was filed by Mr. Bancroft Davis, and the printed Case of Great Britain, with documents, by Lord Tenterden.

The Tribunal made regulation for the filing of the respective Counter-Cases on or before the 15th day of April next ensuing, as required by the Treaty; and for the convening of a special meeting of the Tribunal, if occasion should require; and then, at a second meeting, on the next day, they adjourned until the 15th of June next ensuing, subject to a prior call by the Secretary, if there should be occasion, as provided for in the proceedings at the first Conference.

The record of these, and of all the subsequent Conferences of the Tribunal, is contained in *alternate* Protocols, drawn up both in French and in English, verified by the signatures of the President and Secretary, and of the agents of the two Governments.

In these opening proceedings, that is, at the very

earliest moment possible, signs became visible of the singular want of discretion and good sense of the "enfant terrible," ostentatiously *protocoled* "Lord Chief Justice of England," whom the British Government had placed on the Tribunal.

The vernacular tongue of Count Sclopis was Italian; that of the Baron d'Itajubá, Portuguese; and that of Mr. Stæmpfli, German. Count Sclopis spoke and read English, and Mr. Stæmpfli read it. All the Arbitrators, however, were well acquainted with French; and it was in this language that they communicated with one another, whether in social intercourse or in the discussions of the Tribunal. Thus, we had before us a Tribunal, the members of which did not either of them make use of his own language in their common business; but met, all of them, on the neutral ground of the common diplomatic language of Europe.

In this connection it was that the United States enjoyed their first advantage. Our Government did not need to wait until the organization of the Tribunal to know in what language its proceedings would be conducted; and, in prevision of this fact, it ordered the American "Case" to be translated from the English into French, so as to be presented simultaneously in both languages at the meeting of the Tribunal: the exigency for which was not anticipated, or, if anticipated, was not provided for, by the British Government.

The American "Case" and documents are contained in eight volumes octavo, which consist in all of

5442 pages, as reduced to a common standard, that of the printing by Congress.

The British "Case" and documents fill, in the reprint by Congress, three volumes octavo, consisting of 2823 pages.

Perusal of the American and British Cases, and of their accompanying documents on both sides, brings us to consideration of the peculiarities in the course of argument and trial prescribed by the Treaty.

In effect, the United States were the plaintiffs, and Great Britain the defendant, in a suit at law, to be tried, it is true, before a special tribunal, and determined by conventional rules, but not the less a suit at law for the recovery of damages in reparation of alleged injuries.

In common course, the plaintiff's counsel would open his case and put in his evidence; the defendant's counsel would then open the defense and put in defensive proofs; and, after the close of the testimony on both sides, the defendant's counsel would argue in close for the defense, and then the plaintiff's counsel in final close for the plaintiff.

Here, on the contrary, the defendant's opening argument and defensive proofs went in at the same time as the plaintiff's opening argument and proofs, each under the name of the "Case" of the respective Party.

The British Case, of course, could not answer the American Case, save by conjecture and anticipation founded on common knowledge of the subject-matter.

The respective Counter-Cases of the Parties were to go in together, in like manner, in April, and their respective Arguments in June: so that the Counter-Cases would on each side be response to the previous Cases, and the Arguments to the previous Counter-Cases.

This course of presentation was in no sort prejudicial to the United States, as plaintiffs, and was exceedingly advantageous to Great Britain, as defendant.

THE AMERICAN CASE.

Nevertheless, when our "Case" went in,—that is to say, the opening argument for the United States,—its true character as such was misapprehended in England, where it seemed to be forgotten that the time and place for replying to it were in the British Counter-Case, and not in the newspapers of London or in the British Parliament.

Similar misconception occurred subsequently with regard to the American Argument; the Counsel for Great Britain thinking that he ought to have the opportunity of replying, as will be explained hereafter, and losing sight of the fact that the British Government had already argued the matter three times in "Case," "Counter-Case," and "Argument."

As to the American Case, it seemed to fall into the adversary's camp like a bomb-shell, which rendered every body dumb for a month, and then produced an explosion of clamor, which did not cease for three or four months, and until the final decision of the Tribunal of Arbitration.

The leading journals of England, whether daily or weekly, such as the London Times, Telegraph, and

News, the Saturday Review, the Spectator, the Pall Mall Gazette, the Manchester Guardian, and other British journals generally, are certainly conducted with great ability, and are second, in character and in value, to no others in Europe. In view of which it must be confessed that the outcry which they made against the American Case seemed to me at the time to be altogether unworthy of them and of England.

It was my opinion on reading the American Case for the first time, and is my opinion now, after repeated readings, that it is not only a document of signal ability, learning, and forensic force,—which, indeed, every body admits,—but that it is also temperate in language and dignified in spirit, as becomes any state paper which is issued in the name of the United States.

I do not mean to say that it is so *cold* a document as the British Case. Warmth or coldness of color is a matter of taste, in respect of which the United States have no call to criticise Great Britain, and Great Britain has no right to criticise the United States.

We may presume that, in the exercise of its unquestionable right, the Government of the United States made up its Case in the aim of convincing the Arbitrators, and not with any dominant purpose or special expectation of pleasing Great Britain.

But there is no just cause of exception to the general tenor, spirit, or style of the American Case. Its facts are pertinent; its reasonings are cogent; its conclusions are logical: and in all that is the true explanation of the emotion it occasioned in England.

Intelligent people there, on reading the American Case, then opened their eyes universally to the fact that Great Britain was *about to be tried* before a high court constituted by three neutral Governments. That was not an agreeable subject of reflection. Intelligent Englishmen also, on reading the American Case, began to be uneasily conscious of the strength of the cause of the United States. And that was not an agreeable subject of reflection. For a good cause, in a good court, seemed likely to result in a great international judgment adverse to England.

The specific objections preferred were quite futile. Thus, complaint was made because the Case charged the British Ministers with unfriendliness to the United States for a certain period of the Civil War. But the charge was proved by citing the declarations of those Ministers; it was not, and could not be denied by any candid Englishman; it is admitted by Sir Alexander Cockburn in the dissenting opinion which he filed at the close of the Arbitration. And the charge was pertinent, because it explained the negligent acts of subordinate British authorities, as at Liverpool or Nassau: which acts could not be otherwise explained unless by suggesting a worse imputation, namely, that of hostile insincerity on the part of the Ministers.

If there be any person at the present day, who is inclined to call in question the truth of the foregoing remarks, he is earnestly entreated to read the American Case now, in the light of the *adjudged guilt* of the British Government, and he will then see ample cause to approve the reason, the dignity, and the temper of that Case.

EXPLANATION OF OBJECTIONS TO THE AMERICAN CASE.

The truth undoubtedly is, that discontent with the Treaty itself had much to do in England with objections to the "Case." The British Ministers had negotiated the Treaty in perfect good faith, and in well-founded conviction of its wisdom, of the justice of its provisions, and of its not conflicting with the honor either of Great Britain or of the United States. Parliament had accepted the Treaty without serious opposition, and with but little debate, except on the very trivial *party* question whether it was more or less favorable to Great Britain than the conventions negotiated by Lord Stanley and the Earl of Clarendon. And Great Britain, as a *nation*, had, beyond all peradventure, heartily approved and welcomed the conclusion of the Treaty.

But, on reading the American Case, and reflecting on the constitution of the proposed Tribunal, many Englishmen yielded to a sentiment of undue estimate of *English* law and *English* lawyers, as distinguished from the laws and the lawyers of Continental Europe and of Spanish and Portuguese America. England has good reason to be proud of her legal institutions and of her jurists, and, of late years, she has learned to regard the common law with some abatement of that *fetichism* of devotion which was taught by Coke and by Fortescue. But the statesmen appointed by the three neutral Governments to act as Arbitrators at Geneva, and who, it was clearly seen, would be the effective judges in the cause, were not likely to share the English opinion of the common law of England. And these three Arbitrators were persons outside of the range of the observation, knowledge, or appreciation of most Englishmen, who felt undefined distrust of men whom they did not and could not know as they knew Englishmen and Americans. . Nay, Englishmen were heard to say, in conversation, that they would prefer a tribunal made up of Englishmen and Americans. We shall fully comprehend how strong this sentiment was among average Englishmen, when we remember that expression was given to it in the House of Lords by the Marquess of Salisbury, who, notwithstanding his high intelligence, and the cosmopolitan experience which men of his rank possess, could characterize as *unknown*, and, therefore, as objectionable, an actual Embassador in France, an ex-President of Switzerland, and a Senator and ex-Minister of Italy with fame as a jurist and historian pervading Europe. It was a sentiment which Sir Alexander Cockburn betrayed in his deportment and language at several meetings of the Tribunal.

These, however, were but the transitory incidents of popular emotion and public discussion, and of secondary significance.

AGITATION RESPECTING THE NATIONAL CLAIMS.

But the agitation which soon followed, on the subject of certain of the claims set forth in the Case of the United States, arose at once to national importance. I allude, of course, to what was frequently spoken of as the question of "indirect claims."

The expression is incorrect, and, if admissible as a popular designation, it must not be permitted to produce any misconception of the true question at issue. It would be less inaccurate to speak of them as "claims for indirect or constructive losses or damages," which is the more common phrase in the diplomatic papers; and less inaccurate still to say "remote or consequential losses and damages." But, in truth, none of these expressions are correct, and the use of them has done much to obscure the actual point of controversy, and to divert the public mind into devious paths of argument or conclusion.

When, in the instructions to Mr. Motley of September 25th, 1869, President Grant caused the British Government to be informed, through the Secretary of State, of the nature of the grievances of the United States, he employed the following language:

"The President is not yet prepared to pronounce on the question of the indemnities which he thinks due by Great Britain to individual citizens of the United States for the destruction of their property by rebel cruisers fitted out in the ports of Great Britain.

"Nor is he now prepared to speak of the reparation which he thinks due by the British Government for the larger account of the vast *national* injuries it has inflicted on the United States.

"Nor does he attempt now to measure the relative effect of the various causes of injury, whether by untimely recognition of belligerency, by suffering the fitting out of rebel cruisers, or by the supply of ships, arms, and munitions of war to the Confederates, or otherwise, in whatsoever manner.

"Nor does it fall within the scope of this dispatch to discuss the important changes in the rules of public law, the desirableness of which has been demonstrated by the incidents of the last few years, now under consideration, and which, in view of the maritime prominence of Great Britain and the United States, it would befit them to mature and propose to the other States of Christendom.

"All these are subjects of future consideration, which, when the time for action shall arrive, the President will consider with sincere and earnest desire that all differences between the two nations may be adjusted amicably and compatibly with the honor of each, and to the promotion of future concord between them; to which end he will spare no effort within the range of his supreme duty to the right and interests of the United States."

The British Government was in this way distinctly notified that, in addition to the question of indemnities to individual citizens for the destruction of their property, the United States were entitled to reparation "for the larger account of the vast *national* injuries" inflicted on them as a *Government*.

That the British Government so understood the matter is proved by the tenor of the elaborate responsive paper, styled " Observations," appended to Lord Clarendon's dispatch to Sir Edward Thornton of the ensuing November; and our *national* claims are specifically commented on in those " Observations."

It is immaterial how these *national* losses came afterward to be designated by the title of constructive or indirect; yet such is the fact.

Now, it is perfectly clear that *national* claims are not claims for indirect or constructive loss, any more than individual claims are. In fact, throughout the legal discussions before the Tribunal, the British Government steadily maintained that all the claims of individual citizens for the destruction of their vessels by Confederate cruisers were in the nature of constructive, indirect, remote, and consequential injuries or losses, and, therefore, not recoverable in law, either by the rules of the common law of England or of the civil law as practiced on the Continent. Nothing could more clearly show the inapplicability and equivocation of the phrase "indirect" claims or losses to designate any of the contents of the Treaty of Washington.

Manifestly, while private losses are supposable which may be direct to individual citizens, national losses are supposable which may be direct to the nation. On the other hand, private losses are supposable as well as national, which any jurist or any court would pronounce to be indirect, remote, or consequential in their nature.

All the discussion on this question asserts or admits impliedly that the capture of a private merchant's vessel by a Confederate cruiser inflicted direct loss or damage on the citizen-proprietor. Was not the loss or damage occasioned by the capture of a Government vessel equally a case of direct loss to the *Government?* Most assuredly.

Pursue the inquiry one step further. If, in a war carried on by land between two States, one of them invades the other and devastates the territory thereof, is not that a case of direct injury to the invaded *State?* If the hostilities in question be purely maritime, as in the example of the imperfect or *quasi* war between the United States and France in the closing years of the last century, can it be denied that the injuries done to either nation by such hostilities on the sea involve direct national as well as private injuries?

On first impression, therefore, it might seem that the British Government and British opinion ran wild in the chase of shadows, and combated a creature of mere imagination in quarreling with this part of the American Case at all, and, still more, in contending that on this account Great Britain could be justified in revoking the arbitration agreed upon,—that is, in effect, violating the Treaty.

The Treaty referred to the Tribunal of Arbitration, in terms unequivocal, *all claims of the United States growing out of the acts committed by certain vessels, and generically known as "Alabama Claims."* It might need to go outside of the Treaty into antecedent or contemporaneous diplomatic correspondence in order to ascertain the meaning of the phrase "*Alabama* Claims;" but, in so doing, it would incontrovertibly appear, at every stage of such correspondence, that *national* as well as individual claims were comprehended, and were all confounded together, and, indeed, without mention of individual claims, in the designation of "claims on the part of the United States."

Whether any of the claims so preferred on the part of the United States were for losses indirect or consequential would be an ordinary question of jurisprudence, for the decision of the Tribunal of Arbitration, and could not be a question affecting the integrity or force of the Treaty.

No expression or even intimation of the question of "direct or indirect" appears on the face of the Treaty.

And, in the long diplomatic correspondence which ensued on this subject, it was conclusively demonstrated by Mr. Fish, and was, in effect, admitted by Lord Granville, that no agreement, promise, or understanding existed on the part of the Commissioners to qualify the clear and explicit language of the Treaty.

CAUSE OF THIS AGITATION.

Hence we might well infer or believe that the superficial or apparent question, which so agitated people of high intelligence and practical sense like the English, was not the real or true one. It was not. And, in order to understand the causes of the storm of discussion which broke over England when the tenor of the American Case came to be fully apprehended there, and of the real consternation which seemed to prevail on the subject, it is necessary to take into consideration certain facts wholly independent of the American Case and the Treaty.

On occasion of the rejection by the United States of the Johnson-Clarendon Treaty, with Mr. Sumner's speech as a commentary on that act, England came distinctly to comprehend, what she had been frequently told before but would not believe, that the United States attributed the prolongation of our Civil War largely to her premature recognition of the belligerence of the Confederates, and to the consequent facility of the latter to obtain supplies; and also, though less so, yet in an appreciable degree, to the naval warfare which the Confederates carried on against us from the basis of operations of the ports of Great Britain.

Careful perusal of the instructions to Mr. Motley would have shown that the President of the United States, while persisting to claim reparation for all injuries done by Confederate cruisers, whether to individuals or to the nation, did not insist on the recognition of belligerence as a continuing subject of claim of Great Britain.

Conscious of this distinction, while the American Commissioners would not relinquish claim on account of any thing done by Confederate cruisers, the British Commissioners were content with stipulations of indemnity, which covered all *national* claims of the last category, but did not reach back to claims on account of the unreasonableness and prematurity of the proclamation of the Queen.

That is what is meant by Mr. Bernard in his lecture at Oxford, where he speaks of the *specific* character of the stipulations: they were specific, confined to acts of the Confederate cruisers. And the point is clearly evolved in the debate in the House of Lords on occasion of the presentation of the Treaty, when Lord Russell objected that it was no better for Great Britain than the Johnson-Clarendon Treaty, and Lord Granville replied that it was better, because, while it includes claims on account of acts of cruisers, it does not include claims on account of the Queen's proclamation recognizing the belligerence of the Confederates.

Nevertheless, when, in England, the *argument* of the American Case had been read and pondered,— when it was perceived that this argument imputed to Great Britain *constructive complicity* with the Confederates by reason of the culpable negligence of the British Government to arrest the enterprises of such vessels as the *Alabama*, the *Florida*, and the *Shenandoah*,—and, finally, when it was thus understood that, in preferring claim for all the loss or injury growing out of the acts of those cruisers, whether to the Government or to private citizens, the United States did, in express terms as well as in legal intendment, hold the British Government responsible for prolongation of our Civil War and the cost of its prosecution,— when all these relations of the subject came to be understood, the public mind in England, and especially the commercial mind, recurred at once to the event which constituted at the time the dominant pre-occupation of Europe, namely, the war indemnity of six milliards so recently imposed by Germany on France.

In view of this, a panic terror seemed to seize upon London, similar to what occasionally occurs in New York and other great money centres, producing a state of demonstrative emotion, which, to calm observers outside of such centres, looks like the spasmodic agitation of men who have lost their senses, rather than intelligent human action. Such, indeed, is all panic terror, as exemplified by numerous historical incidents of the contagious influence, both in peace and war, of the most trivial causes and the most absurd illusions.

On the present occasion, London appears to have been shaken and tossed by the intense fear of Great Britain being in turn called upon to pay some indefinite milliards of war indemnity to the United States.

DISCUSSION BETWEEN THE TWO GOVERNMENTS.

The British Government was very slow to take this infection of popular fear and commotion. The American Case was duly filed on the 15th of December. Many copies of it were in the hands of the British Ministers in a few days thereafter. We do not hear of any particular disturbance of mind on the part of the Ministers until the beginning of February, that is, the lapse of six or seven weeks, when the American Minister, General Schenck, telegraphed to Mr. Fish as follows: "London *journals* all demand that the United States shall withdraw claims for indirect damages, as not within intention of treaty. *Ministry alarmed*." To which Mr. Fish responded by telegraph as follows: "There must be no withdrawal of any part of the claim presented. Counsel will argue the case as prepared, unless they show to this Government reasons for a change. The alarm you speak of does not reach us. We are perfectly calm and content to await the award, and do not anticipate repudiation of the Treaty by the other side." And in these two telegrams we have the history of the whole interval of time prior to the next meeting of the Tribunal. Newspapers in England lashed themselves into a "fine frenzy." Ministers and the Parliament, instead of manfully taking a stand at the outset in opposition to the popular current of delusion and passion, got alarmed and lost their heads, and said and did some things not creditable to the British Government. In the United States, on the other hand, sundry persons were officiously over-zealous on the wrong side; the newspaper press was a little *flustered;* and some things were written and published which it would have been better not to write and publish; but the public mind maintained its equilibrium, content, on the whole, to await the progress of the arbitration: while the President, the Secretary of State, with his colleagues of the Cabinet, and the Congress, remained "perfectly calm," standing always on the stipulations of the Treaty, and never believing it would be broken or disregarded by Great Britain.

In my opinion, the contrast at this time between the attitude of the British Government and that of the American Government deserves a few words of commentary.

It is not uncommon in England to suppose and to say that *demagogy*, that is, factious appeal to popular prejudice and passion, is a conspicuous feature of political action in the United States. It seems to be supposed also that demagogy here pleases itself especially with accusations of Great Britain. Meanwhile, it is complacently assumed that self-possession and stability, with unexceptional amiability toward the United States, characterize political action in

Great Britain. I think the absolute reverse of all this is the truth.

In Great Britain the political institutions of the country are indefinite, unwritten, unfixed, without a positive stand-point any where, shifting from day to day; consisting, in form, of Kings, Lords, and Commons, without any visible lines of limitation between them, and resolved to-day into an omnipotent Parliament, one branch of which, the House of Commons, arrogates to itself the character of a constituent national convention to impose on King and Lords any change in the national institutions it sees fit, and assuming to itself the function, by means of a *quasi* committee of its body, to control absolutely the administration, both foreign and domestic, of Great Britain.

This *quasi* committee of the House of Commons, to be sure, has associated with it another *quasi* committee of the House of Lords: which, all together, formerly called Ministers of the Crown, now take to themselves, in the very text of treaties as well as in domestic affairs, the revolutionary title of the " British Government."

But, while the theoretical power of the Crown is nominally exercised by a joint committee of both Houses of Parliament, it is vested, in fact, in the committee of the House of Commons, which, upon all occasions, whether of ordinary administrative matters or of the frequently recurring radical changes in the political institutions of the country, constantly and loudly defies and overbears the House of Lords.

If any simple-minded person in the United States happens to cherish those romantic illusions respecting the constitution of England which he may have acquired from perusal of the Commentaries of Sir William Blackstone, he has but to turn over the leaves of some volume of Hansard's Debates in Parliament, or peruse authoritative disquisitions on the subject, like those of May and of Bagehot, to discover that, in knowledge and reading at least, he has not yet emerged from the mythical epoch of the political history of England.

Now, the submergence of the power of the Crown in Parliament, and of that of Parliament in the House of Commons, and the commitment of all these powers to transitory nominees of the House of Commons, are facts which, combined, have produced the result that *government* in England is at the mercy of every gust of popular passion, every storm of misdirected public opinion, every devious impulse of demagogic agitation,—nothing correspondent to which exists in the United States.

Mr. Gladstone is Prime Minister of Great Britain, —that is to say, of three hundred millions of men, aggregated into various States of Europe, Africa, America, Asia, and Australasia. But he holds all this power at the mere will of a majority of the House of Commons. He must consult their wishes and their prejudices in every act of his political life. If he conceives a great idea, he can not make any thing of it until after he shall have driven it into the heads of three or four hundred country gentlemen, which are not always easily *perforable* either by eloquence or by reason. And during the progress of all great measures, including especially foreign negotiations, which require to be left undisturbed in their progress from germination to maturity, he is subject to be goaded almost to madness every day by vicious interpellations, not only on the part of members of the Opposition, but even his own supporters in the House of Commons.

How different is the spectacle of government in the United States! Here, the President,—that is, the Prime Minister of the sovereign people,—is placed in power for a fixed period of time, during which he is politically independent of faction, and can look at the temporary passions of the hour with calmness, so as to judge them at their true value, and accept or reject their voice according to the dictates of public duty and the command of his conscience. Neither he nor any of the members of his Cabinet are subject to be badgered by factious or unreasonable personal interrogation in either house of Congress.

Moreover, the House of Representatives does not presume to set itself up as the superior either of the President or of the Senate. Nor is the Senate in the condition of being terrified from the discharge of its duty by threats on the part of the President or of the House of Representatives to subjugate its free will at any moment by thrusting into it a batch of twenty new administration Senators. Least of all does the House of Representatives presume to possess and exercise the powers of a constituent national convention, to change in its discretion the constitution of the United States.

Thus it was that, in the matter of the discussion of this Treaty, Mr. Gladstone and the other Ministers were tossed to and fro on the surging waves of public opinion, and pestered from day to day in Parliament, while solicitously engaged in reflecting how best to keep faith with the United States and at the same time do no prejudice to Great Britain. If, at that period, the Ministers said in debate any thing unwise, any thing not strictly true or just,—Mr. Gladstone did, but Lord Granville did not,—let it not be remembered against them personally, but charged to the uncontrollable difficulties of their position, and the signal defectiveness and intrinsic weakness of the organic institutions of Great Britain.

During all that period of earnest discussion on both sides of the ocean, it was to me, as an American, matter of the highest thankfulness and gratulation and patriotic pride, to see the Government of the United States,—President, Secretary of State, Cabinet, Congress,—continue in the even tenor of their public duty, calm, unruffled, self-possessed, as the stars in heaven. The Executive of the United States is, it is true, by its very nature, a thoughtful and self-contained power. Congress, on the other hand, is the field of debate and the place where popular passions come into evidence, as the winds in the cave of Æolus. But, on this occasion, no more debate occurred in either House than that least possible expression of opinion, which was necessary to show accord with the

Executive. Even the Opposition, to its honor be it said, conducted itself with commendable reserve and consideration. How different from all this was the spectacle exhibited by the British Parliament!

ENGLISH MISCONCEPTION OF AMERICAN SENTIMENT.

I contradict, with equal positiveness, the suggestion that demagogic agitation in the United States feeds itself largely on alleged hatred of Great Britain. I think topics of international reproach are more common in England than here. The steady current of emigration from England, Scotland, and Ireland to the United States, and especially at the present time from England, is not a grateful subject of contemplation in Great Britain. England perceives, but not with perfect contentedness, that the British race in America bids fair soon to exceed in numbers and in power the British race in Europe. And, above all, the gradually increasing force of those factions or parties in Great Britain, which demand progressive enlargement of the basis of suffrage, equal distribution of representation, vote by ballot, the separation of Church and State, subdivision of the great properties in land, cessation of hereditary judicial and political power, intellectual and social elevation of the disinherited classes,—I say such parties or factions, in appealing to the institutions of the United States as a model, provoke criticism of those institutions on the part of the existing depositaries of property and political power. Owing to these, and other causes which might be indicated, it seems to me that the United

States encounter more criticism in Great Britain than Great Britain does in the United States.

Moreover, it should be borne in mind that much of the inculpation of Great Britain which is perceived in the United States proceeds from British immigrants,—largely Irish, but in part Scottish and English,—who, like other Europeans, are but too prone to come here with all their native political prejudices clinging to them; who not seldom hate the Government of their native land; and who, of course, need time to cease to be Europeans in spirit and to become simply Americans. And it would not be without interest in this relation to see how many of such persons, in the newspaper press or elsewhere, say or do things tending to cause it to be supposed that opinion in the United States is hostile to Great Britain.

There is one other class of facts which it is proper to state in this relation, and particularly proper for me to state.

The successful revolution of the thirteen Colonies was an event most unacceptable, of course, to England. We, the victors in that contest, should not murmur if resentful memories thereof lingered for some time in the breasts of the defeated party. I think, however, such feelings have ceased to manifest themselves in England. It is to quite other causes, in my opinion, that we are to attribute the successive controversies between the two countries, in which, as it seems to me, the greater wrong has in each case been on the side of England. I think we did not afford her sufficient cause of complaint for continuing in hostile oc-

D

cupation of the Northwestern Territory for so many years after we had made peace. I think she was wrong in issuing the notorious Orders in Council, and in the visitation of our ships and impressment of our seamen, which morally constrained us, after exhausting all other means of redress, to have recourse to war. I think she was wrong in contending that that war extinguished the rights of coast fishery assured to us by the Treaty of Independence. I think she was wrong in the controversy on the subject of colonial trade, which attained so much prominence during the Presidency of John Quincy Adams. I think she was wrong in attempting to set up the fictitious Mosquito Kingdom in Central America. I think she was wrong in the so-called San Juan Question. And so of other subjects of difference between the two Governments.

Now, it has happened to me, in the course of a long public life, to be called on to deal officially, either in Congress, in the Cabinet, or at the Bar, with many of these points of controversy between the two Governments, of which it suffices to mention for example three, namely: 1, the Question of British Enlistments; 2, the Hudson's Bay Company; and 3, the Alabama Claims.

In regard to the first of these questions, the United States, and the persons who administered the Government, were so clearly right that, although the British Government, in its Case, improvidently brought into controversy at Geneva, by way of counter-accusation, the general conduct of the United States during the war between Great Britain and Russia, and although we replied by charging in response that the only violations of neutrality committed in the United States during that war were committed by Great Britain herself, yet in the subsequent discussions not a word of self-justification on this point was preferred by the British Government.

In regard to the second of the questions, a member of Parliament [Mr. Hughes], in ignorance of the facts, it is to be presumed, undertook to impugn the conduct of the Counsel of the United States, and to draw inferences therefrom prejudicial to the conduct of the United States in the Arbitration at Geneva. In response to this complaint, it suffices to say that, on occasion of a settlement of the claims of the Hudson's Bay Company and of its shadow, the Puget's Sound Agricultural Company, by mixed commission, under the treaty of July, 1863, it devolved on me, in behalf of the United States, to assert, and to prove to the satisfaction of the Commission, that the pretensions of the Hudson's Bay Company were scandalously unjust, and founded on premises of exaggeration and usurpation injurious to Great Britain and to the Canadian Dominion, as well as to the United States. I have no reason to regret or qualify any thing said or done by me in that affair.

As to the third of these questions, namely, the *Alabama* Claims, it seems difficult to comprehend how persistent demand of redress on the part of the United States can be complained of by any candid Englishman *now*, when the judgment of the Tribunal of Arbitration establishes the fact of the long denial of justice by Great Britain in this behalf,—a fact admitted also by so prejudiced a person as Sir Alexander Cockburn, who speaks as ["in some sense" at least] "the representative of Great Britain."

I confidently maintain, therefore, that neither the British Government nor the people of Great Britain had any just cause, in the course of these transactions, to find fault with the spirit, temper, or language either of the Government or the Agent or Counsel of the United States. To the contrary of this, it seems to me that on our side alone is the good cause of complaint in these respects.

ATTITUDE OF THE AMERICAN GOVERNMENT.

As respects the deportment of the two *Governments* in this crisis, certain it is that the conduct of that of Great Britain, in resting upon the American Case for nearly seven weeks, and then abruptly breaking out, in the Queen's speech from the throne and in debate in Parliament, with objections to that Case, without previous statement thereof in diplomatic communication, was uncourteous toward the United States.

The diplomatic discussion which ensued, beginning with Lord Granville's note of February 3, 1872, and terminating with the dispatch of Mr. Fish of April 16, 1872, may now be read, not with composure only, but with supreme satisfaction, by any citizen of the United States. The Secretary of State [Mr. Fish] demonstrates to conviction the utter baselessness of the pretension of the British Government that the so-called indirect claims were not within the letter or spirit of the Treaty of Washington. And he repels throughout, peremptorily but dispassionately, the call of the British Government on the United States to withdraw this class of claims from the consideration of the Tribunal. In fine, the position of the United States is plainly expressed in different parts of the dispatches of Mr. Fish, as follows:

"They [the United States] desire to maintain the jurisdiction of the Tribunal of Arbitration over all the unsettled claims, in order that, being judicially decided, and the questions of law involved therein being adjudicated, all questions connected with or arising out of the *Alabama* Claims, or 'growing out of the acts' of the cruisers, may be forever removed from the possibility of disturbing the perfect harmony of relations between the two countries. . . .

"What the rights, duties, and true interests of both the contending nations, and of all nations, demand shall be the extent, and the measure of liability and damages under the Treaty, is a matter for the supreme determination of the Tribunal established thereby.

"Should that august Tribunal decide that a State is not liable for the indirect or consequential results of an accidental or unintentional violation of its neutral obligations, the United States will unhesitatingly accept the decision.

"Should it, on the other hand, decide that Great Britain is liable to this Government for such consequential results, they have that full faith in British observance of its engagements to expect a compliance with the judgment of the Tribunal, which a solemn Treaty between the two Powers has created in order to remove and adjust all complaints and claims on the part of the United States."

The American Government could not avoid feeling that the public discussion, which the British Ministers had seen fit to excite, or, at any rate, to aggravate, and "the discourteous tone and minatory intimations of the Ministry," imposed on the United States a different line of action from that, which might have been adopted by them in response to a calm presentation by the British Government of its construction of the Treaty.

In this relation there is another class of facts which, as it seems to me, deserves mention.

Of the five American Commissioners engaged in the negotiation of the Treaty of Washington, two, the Secretary of State [Mr. Fish] and our Minister at London [General Schenck], were officially occupied in discussing the question on the American Case raised by the British Government. The published dispatches show with what signal ability they discharged this delicate duty. Meanwhile, the three other Commissioners, Mr. Justice Nelson, Mr. Hoar, and Mr. Williams, although *impliedly* accused on the other side of taking some advantage of the unsophisticated innocence and simplicity of the British Commissioners, yet maintained perfect self-control in the matter, speaking only when officially called upon to speak, and otherwise leaving the subject where it belonged,—in the hands of their Government.

The conduct, on the other hand, of some of the British Commissioners was less reserved than that of the American Commissioners. Professor Bernard got completely off the track of reason and sense in a lecture which he delivered at Oxford. Sir Stafford Northcote let off a very inconsiderate speech at Exeter. And Sir Edward Thornton made a not very considerate one at New York. But Earl de Grey and Ripon, who had now become Marquess of Ripon, deported himself with admirable dignity. It was, indeed, wittily said, or reported to have been said, by Mr. Lowe, that Lord Ripon was going about very sick at the stomach of a marquisate, which he would be glad to throw up; but the reproach was wholly undeserved. Lord Ripon manfully maintained silence while to speak would have been unwise; when at length it became expedient to speak, he did so with discretion and with judiciousness, beyond what appeared in the speeches of some other members of the Government.

ACTION OF THE AMERICAN AGENT AND COUNSEL.

Whilst all these discussions were going on in Great Britain and the United States, we, the Agent and Counsel of the United States, were busily occupied, partly at Washington but chiefly at Paris, in the study of the British Case and the preparation of the American Counter-Case. We had fixed on Paris for our head-quarters, as a neutral city, as a great centre of international jurisprudence and diplomacy, and as a place in easy communication with London and with Washington.

From this ground of vantage we could observe and estimate correctly the current of discussion in America, in Great Britain, and on the Continent of Europe.

Speaking for myself, at least, let me say, it appeared to me that much of what was being said in England, whether in Parliament or in the Press, was unseasonable or indiscreet; much of it factious toward the British Government itself; much of it disrespectful to the American Government; but none of it of any ultimate importance or consequence in regard to either Government, for the following reasons:

1. Both Governments sincerely desired peace. Great Britain could never have retreated from the Arbitration in violation of the Treaty, whatever the Press might say, and whoever should be in power as Minister.

2. Freedom of debate is essential to freedom of institutions. To be sure, the Press in Great Britain, and somewhat, but less so, in the United States, is prone to take upon itself rather lofty airs, and to speak of public affairs quite absolutely, as if it were the Government. But nobody is deceived by this, not even the Press itself. We, the English-speaking nations, thank heaven, possess the capability of living in the atmosphere of oral and written debate. It was safe to predict that howmuchsoever Mr. Gladstone and Lord Granville might feel annoyed by the din of words around them, it would not induce them to break faith with the United States.

3. It was not the voice of the *English* Press which could seriously affect us. We looked rather to the state of opinion in the French, German, and Italian speaking countries of Europe, which, on the whole, though differing as to the legal right of the United States to recover on the national claims, yet decisively agreed with us in affirming that those claims were

comprehended within the scope of the Treaty as maintained by the United States.

What Europe dreaded, what all European opinion sought to prevent, was a *rupture* between Great Britain and the United States, to disturb the money-market of Europe, and impede the payment by France of the indemnity due to Germany. And all men saw that the United States must and would resent the refusal by Great Britain to observe the stipulations of the Treaty of Washington.

PRESENTATION OF COUNTER-CASES.

Such were the circumstances, in the presence of which arrived the time, namely, the 15th of April, at which the two Governments were to file at Geneva their respective Counter-Cases.

The British Government was so solicitous to fulfill on its part all the stipulations of the Treaty, that it caused special inquiry to be made whether the American Government had any objection to Great Britain filing her Counter-Case without prejudice to her position regarding consequential damages; to which Mr. Fish replied that the British Government was bound to file its Counter-Case, but its doing so would not prejudice any position it had taken, nor affect any position of the United States.

Accordingly, on the 15th of April, the Counter-Cases of Great Britain and the United States were duly filed, with express reservation of all the rights of both Governments.

The British Counter-Case, consisting of four volumes folio, contains little new matter, being in part, at least, defensive argument in response to the American "Case."

The American Counter-Case, consisting of two volumes folio, replies argumentatively to the British "Case," and brings forward a large body of documentary proofs, responsive to matters contained in that "Case," which, although utterly foreign to the question at issue, required to be met, because considered material by Great Britain, namely, allegations of default on the part of the United States in the execution of their own neutrality laws, to the prejudice of other Governments.

The introduction of all this matter into the British Case, the iteration of it in the British Counter-Case and the British Argument, and the extreme prominence given to it, as we shall hereafter see, by the British Arbitrator, serve to illustrate the singular unreasonableness and injustice of the angry complaints emitted in England against the American Case.

The American Case contains no suggestion which is not strictly pertinent to the issues raised by the Treaty. It discusses the conduct of the British Government relatively to the United States during our Civil War, with strict application to the "*Alabama* Claims." It charges that, in those transactions, the British Government was guilty of culpable omission to observe the requirements of the law of nations as respects the United States, and with responsible negligence in the non-execution of the neutrality laws of

Great Britain. That was the very question presented by the Treaty.

Great Britain professed to be so much offended by the character of certain of the proofs adduced in the American Case,—rigorously pertinent to the question as all those proofs were,—that she would not suffer any appropriate answer to those proofs to be brought forward in her Counter-Case or in her Argument: it was not compatible with self-respect,—it would be giving dignity to undignified arguments,—we were told by the British Press. Meanwhile, the very matter which the British Government could not condescend to notice was both material and important to such a degree as very much to inflame the temper and exercise the ingenuity of Sir Alexander Cockburn, the "representative" of Great Britain at Geneva.

Now, the American Case, if conceived in any other spirit than that of just and fair exposition of the precise issue,—question, that is, whether the British Government had or had not incurred responsibility for its want of due diligence in the matter of Confederate cruisers fitted out in the ports of Great Britain,—I say, if the American Government, in the preparation of its Case, had not been animated by the spirit of perfect fairness and justness, it *might* have gone into the inquiry of the political conduct of Great Britain in other times, and with reference to other nations, in the view of imputing to her *habitual* disregard of the law of nations in illustration of her present conduct toward the United States. We might have charged that, while her statesmen contend that they could do nothing outside of an Act of Parliament, they had no such Act until 1819, and were therefore, prior to that time, confessedly impotent, and we might have added willfully so, to observe the duties of neutrality; we might have scrutinized her national history to select conspicuous examples of her acts of violence, in disregard of the law of nations, against numerous States, including ourselves; we might have appealed to every volume of international law in existence, from the time of Grotius to this day, and cited page after page to the conclusion of the unjust international policy of Great Britain; and we might have argued from all this to infer intentional omission of the British Government to prevent the escape of the *Alabama* and the *Florida*.

But such arguments, you will say, would have been forced, remote, of doubtful relevance, and of a nature offensive to England. Be it so: they would, if you please, have been irrelevant, impertinent, offensive. And no such arguments are found in the American Case.

But such are the arguments which pervade the British Case, Counter-Case, and Argument, and the opinions of the British member of the Tribunal. Instead of defending its own conduct in the matter at issue, the British Government travels out of the record to find fault with the conduct of the United States at other times, and with respect to other nations. It presumes to take upon itself the function of personating Spain, Portugal, Nicaragua, and to drag before the Tribunal at Geneva controversies between us and other States, with which that Tribunal had no possible concern,—which it could not pretend to judge,—and of such obvious irrelevancy and impertinence that not one of the Arbitrators condescended to notice them except Sir Alexander Cockburn.

The presentation in the British Case of considerations of this order, worthless and absurd as argument, and wantonly offensive to the United States, was, in my judgment, an outrageous act, compared with which, in possible susceptibility of blame, there is nothing to be found in any of the affirmative documents presented by the American Government.

It was the cause of a singularly perverse incident, namely, complaint of the British Press against the American Argument for imputed *unkindness* in alluding to subjects, which had been forced upon our attention by the British Case.

I mention these circumstances for the purpose of showing how relatively unjust it was to impute offensiveness of spirit and language to the American Case in view of the much more objectionable things in the British Case; and for the further purpose of pertinently stating that it was undignified for Great Britain to complain of the manner in which the Agent or Counsel of the United States might see fit to argue our cause, as it would be for the American Government to undertake to prescribe limits of discretion in this respect to the Agent or Counsel of Great Britain.

Thus, the 15th of April, looked forward to with so much apparent dread by the British Government, passed away, leaving the great question unsettled, in what manner ultimately to deal with the claim for national losses preferred by the United States.

NEGOTIATIONS FOR A SUPPLEMENTAL TREATY.

A new series of events then happened, which occupied the period intervening between the 15th of April and the 15th of June.

It occurred to the two Governments that the difficulty might be disposed of by the exchange of diplomatic notes, which, in laying down a definite rule of reciprocal international right on the subject of such losses, should reserve or leave unimpaired the present pretensions of both Governments. The British Government would not admit that it was the intention of the Treaty to cover national losses; the United States insisted that it was, and refused to do any act incompatible with this construction of the Treaty; and, therefore, they would not withdraw any part of the American Case, nor disavow the opinion that it was within the province of the Arbitrators to consider all the claims, and to determine the liability of Great Britain for all the claims, which had been put forward by the United States. But the American Government had not asked for pecuniary damages in its "Case" on account of that part of the claims called the indirect losses; it only desired a judgment thereon, which would remove them for all future time as a cause of difference between the two Governments. To hold that this class of claims was not disposed of by the Treaty,—that is, was not a subject for the consideration of the Tribunal of Arbitration,—was to infer that they remained open and unadjusted, and susceptible of being hereafter brought forward anew by the United States as an object of reclamation against Great Britain. One great inducement to the Treaty would thus be defeated, namely, the establishment of perfect concord and peace. In view of which it was thought expedient to endeavor to adjust the present dispute by informal stipulations on the part of the two Governments.

This well-intentioned effort failed, because of the persistent contention of the British Government that the Treaty excluded from the Arbitration the claims for national losses advanced by the United States.

Further reflection on the subject satisfied the American Government that nothing short of a new treaty could dispose of the question on the premises of the pending negotiation, it being clear that the President of the United States could not of himself *withdraw* claims which were in his opinion justified by the Treaty of Washington.

Thereupon the President requested of the Senate an expression of their disposition in regard to advising and consenting to the formal adoption of an article of treaty proposed by the British Government, to the effect of stipulating that he would make no claim on the part of the United States in respect of the so-called indirect losses before the Tribunal of Arbitration, in consideration of an agreement between the two Governments, the essence of which was set forth in a preamble to the effect that

"Such indirect claims as those for national losses stated in the Case presented on the part of the Government of the United States . . . should not be admitted in principle as growing out of the acts committed by particular vessels, alleged to have been enabled to commit depredations on the shipping of a belligerent by reason of such want of due diligence in the performance of neutral obligations as that which is imputed by the United States to Great Britain:"

which proposed agreement the preamble proceeds to state, in the form of two separate declarations,—one by Great Britain and one by the United States,—each of them intelligible only by reference to previous parts of the preamble: the whole to the conclusion that the President shall make no claim, on the part of the United States, in respect of the indirect claims as aforesaid, before the Tribunal of Arbitration at Geneva.

The Senate, thinking that the recitals in the preamble were not sufficiently explicit to furnish to the United States satisfactory basis of transaction, proposed the following substitute:

"Whereas both Governments adopt for the future the principle that claims for remote or indirect losses should not be admitted as the result of failure to observe neutral obligations, so far as to declare that it will hereafter guide the conduct of both Governments in their relations with each other. Now, therefore," etc.

But the Senate's redaction of the article rendered its meaning too clear to be agreeable to the British Government, which, as was shrewdly said of it in Paris at the time, doubted whether release from claim of reparation for the present wrong done by Great

Britain to the United States might not be purchased too dearly by conceding to the United States, in consideration thereof, indefinite and unlimited exemption from responsibility for wrongs of the same nature to be inflicted in all future time by the United States on Great Britain.

Further interchange of dispatches on this subject followed, the British Government insisting on modification of the terms of arrangement proposed by the Senate.

But Congress had now adjourned. The 15th of June was impending, on which day the United States must of necessity present their final argument or lose their hold on the Treaty. If, at the commencement of the difficulty, the British Government had proposed to the American Government to agree to postpone the proceedings of the Tribunal and take time for negotiation in the usual way, a new treaty might have been concluded as contemplated by the two Governments. Such a treaty, requiring careful consideration of phraseology, with discussion and explanations regarding the same, could not be concluded in haste by means of telegraphic communication between London and Washington.

The spectacle exhibited by the two Governments at this time was one of profound interest to the whole world. They were inspired by friendly sentiments on each side. They differed in regard to the construction of a treaty which neither desired to break. Diplomatic correspondence had failed to bring them into concord of opinion. They endeavored to reconcile this difference by supplemental treaty. Only a few weeks remained in which to negotiate; and the parties were separated by thousands of miles of ocean. It was necessary, therefore, to negotiate, if at all, by telegraph,—an operation quite as novel as had been that of conducting the business of government in France by means of pigeons or balloons during the siege of Paris. But, before it was possible for the parties to conclude a treaty by telegraph, the fatal day arrived, greatly to the embarrassment of the British Government.

PRESENTATION OF ARGUMENTS FOR THE UNITED STATES.

For the course of the United States in this exigency was plain before them: it was to present their final Argument to the Tribunal of Arbitration, in conformity with their own conception of their rights, just as if there were no controversy on the point between them and Great Britain.

The President of the United States was immovably fixed in the purpose not to withdraw the controverted claims, nor to abstain from making claim before the Tribunal in respect to the so-called indirect losses, except in consideration of a new treaty regarding the same, satisfactory to himself and to the Senate of the United States.

In a dispatch of the Secretary of State to the Minister at London, of the 28th of May, 1872, the inducement and object of the United States, in persisting to retain these claims before the Tribunal, are summarily stated as follows:

1. "The right under the Treaty to present them.
2. "To have them disposed of and removed from further controversy.
3. "To obtain a decision either for or against the liability of a neutral for claims of that description.
4. "If the liability of a neutral for such claims is admitted in the future, then to insist on payment by Great Britain for those of the past.
5. "Having a case against Great Britain to have the same principle applied to it that may in the future be invoked against the United States.".

Of these considerations, the last four, it is obvious, are the complete justification of the insertion of our national claims in the Treaty and of their presentation in the "Case."

Hence the duty of the Agent and Counsel of the United States, having charge of the judicial investigation pending before the Tribunal of Arbitration, remained the same in the interval between December 15th, 1871, and June 15th, 1872, whatever diplomatic discussions or negotiations might be going on between the two Governments. Our instructions were definite and peremptory, as the British Government well understood, to prepare the Counter-Case for the United States, and the final Argument, on the premises of the Treaty as construed by the United States and as explained in the American Case. Our Counter-Case was prepared accordingly, as already stated, and filed in English and in French before the Tribunal. And in like manner we prepared our final Argument.

This Argument, consisting of an octavo volume of 495 pages, after discussing fully the various questions of fact and of law involved in the submission to arbitration, proceeds to examine the particular claims, national as well as individual,—to maintain the jurisdiction of the Tribunal over both classes of claims,—and to argue the nature and degree of the responsibility of Great Britain to the United States in the premises. In fine, the Argument is co-extensive with the "Case."

We repaired to Geneva in due time, and at the meeting of the Tribunal on the 15th we presented our Argument as required by the Treaty, and, for the better information of the Tribunal, in French as well as in English. That is to say, the Government of the United States, through the means of its official Agent, complied with that last command of the Treaty of Washington, in virtue of which the Tribunal of Arbitration became formally seized and possessed of all our claims, national as well as private, precisely as if no controversy on the subject existed between the two Governments. The United States were in condition to invoke the judgment of the Tribunal, whether Great Britain appeared or not; for Counsel had ample authority of legal doctrine at hand to show that the Tribunal would have power to act even in the absence of Great Britain.

In the anticipation of this contingency, the British Government requested that of the United States to concur in making a joint application to the Tribunal for an adjournment of eight months, in order to afford to the two Governments sufficient time for further negotiation. Mr. Fish replied that the Government of the United States had no reason to desire such adjournment, although the Government intended, and instructed its Agent, to assent to a motion for adjournment on the part of Great Britain, provided the British Argument were filed in good faith, without offensive notice, or other objectionable accompaniment.

Thus it became necessary for the British Government to decide for itself how to act in the premises. The course adopted by it was to withhold its Argument, and to file a statement, setting forth the recent negotiations for the solution of the difficulty between the two Governments, and the hope that, if time were afforded, such a solution might be found practicable; and thereupon to move an adjournment of eight months, with reserve of all rights in the event of an agreement not being finally arrived at, as expressed in the note which accompanied the British Counter-Case.

DECISION OF THE ARBITRATORS RESPECTING NATIONAL LOSSES.

These acts having been performed, the Arbitrators adjourned, first to the 17th, and then to the 19th of June, in order to afford time for reflection to themselves and to the two Governments.

It will be taken for granted that in the interval between the 15th and the 19th of June communications by telegraph passed between the respective Agents and their Governments, and consultations took place between the Counsel of both sides and the respective Agents, either orally or in writing, and, with more or less formality, among the Arbitrators, the result of which was announced by Count Sclopis as follows:

"The Arbitrators do not propose to express or imply any opinion upon the point thus in difference between the two Governments as to the interpretation or effect of the Treaty, but it seems to them obvious that the substantial object of the adjournment must be to give the two Governments an opportunity of determining whether the claims in question shall or shall not be submitted to the decision of the Arbitrators, and that any difference between the two Governments on this point may make the adjournment unproductive of any useful effect, and, after a delay of many months, during which both nations may be kept in a state of painful suspense, may end in a result which it is to be presumed both Governments would equally deplore, that of making this arbitration wholly abortive. This being so, the Arbitrators think it right to state that, after the most careful perusal of all that has been urged on the part of the Government of the United States in respect of these claims, they have arrived, individually and collectively, at the conclusion that these claims do not constitute, upon the principles of international law applicable to such cases, good foundation for an award of compensation or computation of damages between nations; and should, upon such principles, be wholly excluded from the consideration of the Tribunal in making its award, even if there were no disagreement between the two Governments as to the competency of the Tribunal to decide thereon. With a view to the settlement of the other claims, to the consideration of which by the Tribunal no exception has been taken on the part of Her Britannic Majesty's Government, the Arbitrators have thought it desirable to lay before the parties this expression of the views they have formed upon the question of public law involved, in order that, after this declaration by the Tribunal, it may be considered by the Government of the United States whether any course can be adopted respecting the first-mentioned claims which would relieve the Tribunal from the necessity of deciding upon the present application of Her Britannic Majesty's Government."

Count Sclopis added that it was the intention of the Tribunal that this statement should be considered for the present to be confidential,—that is, subject to the discretion of either of the two Governments.

But what is the "question of public law involved?" Is it the question of claim for indirect or consequential damages, as argued by the British Government? By no means.

Observe, no suggestion of any distinction between direct and indirect claims is to be found in the declaration of the Arbitrators. And their declaration can not be explained by reference to any such order of ideas.

The significant words are: "These claims do not constitute, upon the principles of international law applicable to such cases, good foundation for an award of compensation or computation of damages between nations."

Why do they not? Because they are indirect? Because they are consequential? No such objection is intimated.

But although, in making this declaration, a mere conclusion of mind, the Arbitrators abstained at the time from assigning any reasons for such conclusion, yet they supplied this omission subsequently, as we shall plainly see when we come to review the *ensemble* of all the acts of the Tribunal. We shall then be able to appreciate the importance and value of this declaration to the United States.

The Counsel of the United States advised the acceptance of this declaration by the Government, as follows:

"We are of opinion that the announcement this day made by the Tribunal must be received by the United States as determinative of its judgment on the question of public law involved, as to which the United States have insisted on taking the opinion of the Tribunal. We advise, therefore, that it should be submitted to, as precluding the propriety of further insisting upon the claims covered by this declaration of the Tribunal, and that the United States, with a view of maintaining the due course of the arbitration on the other claims without adjournment, should announce to the Tribunal that the said claims covered by its opinion will not be further insisted upon before the Tribunal by the United States, and may be excluded from all consideration by the Tribunal in making its award."

In response, the Secretary of State communicated the determination of the President, as follows:

"I have laid your telegrams before the President, who directs me to say that he accepts the declaration of the Tribunal as its judgment upon a question of public law, which he had felt that the interests of both Governments required should be decided, and for the determination of which he had felt it important to present the claims referred to for the purpose of taking the opinion of the Tribunal.

"This is the attainment of an end which this Government had in view in the putting forth of those claims. We had no desire for a pecuniary award, but desired an expression by the Tribunal as to the liability of a neutral for claims of that character. The President, therefore, further accepts the opinion and advice of the Counsel as set forth above, and authorizes the announcement to the Tribunal that he accepts their declaration as determinative of their judgment upon the important question of public law as to which he had felt it his duty to seek the expression of their opinion; and that, in accordance with such judgment and opinion, from henceforth he regards the claims set forth in the Case presented on the part of the United States for loss in the transfer of the American commercial marine to the British flag, the enhanced payment of insurance, and the prolongation of the war, and the addition of a large sum to the cost of the war and the suppression of the Rebellion, as adjudicated and disposed of; and that, consequently, they will not be further insisted upon before the Tribunal by the United States, but are henceforth excluded from its consideration by the Tribunal in making its award."

This conclusion was announced to the Tribunal by the Agent of the United States on the 25th of June in the following words:

"The declaration made by the Tribunal, individually and collectively, respecting the claims presented by the United States for the award of the Tribunal for, first, the losses in the transfer of the American commercial marine to the British flag; second, the enhanced payment of insurance; and, third, the prolongation of the war, and the addition of a large sum to the cost of the war and the suppression of the Rebellion, is accepted by the President of the United States as determinative of their judgment upon the important question of public law involved."

On the 27th, the British Agent announced the acquiescence of his Government in this arrangement, withdrew his motion of adjournment, and filed the British Argument.

And in this manner the controversy, which for so many months had engrossed the attention of the two Governments, was finally disposed of as the Government of the United States had constantly contended it should be [unless otherwise settled by treaty],—that is, by the declaration of the judgment or opinion of the Arbitrators, in such form as to constitute, in effect, a rule of law, morally binding on Great Britain and the United States.

The President of the Tribunal, Count Sclopis, then proceeded to pronounce an appropriate and well-written discourse, expressing satisfaction at the removal of all obstacles to the free action of the Tribunal, and commenting on the political relations of the Treaty of Washington, preparatory to the consideration of the other questions submitted to the Arbitrators.

SEAT OF THE ARBITRATION.

And here, before proceeding to explain and to discuss the subsequent acts of the Tribunal, it seems convenient to pause, in order to speak of the scene of action and of the Tribunal, to which the eyes of all nations were attracted, and especially those of the people of England and of America.

It was most fit and proper to select Switzerland as the country, and Geneva as the city, in which to hold the sessions of the Tribunal.

In fact, Switzerland, at the same time that it is the land of hospitality, inviting the frequentation of all the world by its picturesque scenery, the beauty and sublimity of its lakes and mountains, is also the land of neutrality *par excellence*. No other country possesses in the same degree these qualities conjoined. In no other country was it possible to avoid all invidious local suspicion, and to be exempt from any possible political influence foreign to the objects of the Arbitration.

The selection was peculiarly agreeable to the United States, by reason of the striking similarity between our institutions and those of Switzerland. Both Governments cultivate a policy of international neutrality: the one, by reason of its isolation and remoteness from the Old World, and the other because of its geographical position in the midst of the great military Powers of Europe. Both Governments are federal; and Switzerland, not content with those modifications of her system of government adopted in the year 1848, which did so much to assimilate her political organization to that of the United States, now manifests the purpose to amend that Constitution so as to make it still more like to ours. In both countries the force of public life pervades society like the blood in the human system, so that every citizen is an active member of the Republic. Hence it is impossible to an intelligent American to avoid entertaining warm sympathy for the Swiss Confederation.

Geneva is a cosmopolitan city, — situated in the very heart of Europe,—distinguished for the intelligence of its inhabitants and their love of liberty. It is *city*, in respect of the commodities of life: it is *country*, in so far as regards the locality and the surrounding natural objects, Lake Leman, the Jura, and the Alps.

The Federal Government, as well as that of the Canton of Geneva, appreciated the honor of being the seat of this great international Tribunal, and did not fail to welcome most cordially the two Governments, their Agents and their Counsel, by conspicuous manifestations of political as well as of personal consideration. The Cantonal Government at Geneva hastened to provide suitable accommodations for the Tribunal in the Hôtel de Ville of that city; it afforded to the members of the Tribunal and to 'the representatives of the two Governments access to numerous official exhibitions and entertainments; and, at a suitable time, it made for us a special festival at Geneva, as the Federal Government did at Interlaken and at Berne.

Switzerland, and Geneva especially, looking at the several acts of arbitration provided by the Treaty of Washington as constituting great steps in the progress of public peace, welcomed us the more heartily because of the recent organization there of a society, whose objects are defined by its title of "Comité International de Secours aux Militaires Blessés." This society had acquired universal respect by its acts of disinterested philanthropy in the late war between Germany and France. Its symbol of the red cross had been the harbinger of relief to many a suffering victim of battle. It was organized under the Presidency of that General Dufour who, in 1847, had led to victory the forces of Switzerland against the Secession [Sonderbund] Cantons. And men could not fail to note the coincidence, when they saw this great Tribunal of Arbitration organized under the auspices of the victorious commander of our own Union forces [General Grant], as the International Commission for the Succor of the Wounded had been under the auspices of the veteran General Dufour. It was impressive to see the greatest Generals of the two countries laboring to diminish the chances and lighten the evils of war.

The Tribunal of Arbitration occupied the same hall in the Hôtel de Ville which had just before been occupied by the Society for the Succor of the Wounded: a room of moderate dimensions, but adequate to the purpose, fitted up with elegance and good taste, not, however, specially for the Commission or Tribunal, but for ordinary uses of the City or Canton, indicated by its title "Salle des Conférences."

The Hôtel de Ville is a structure in the Florentine style of architecture, situated on the summit of the old Geneva, and which is occupied both by municipal officers of the City and by the executive and legislative authorities of the Canton.

COUNT FREDERIC SCLOPIS.

Here, then, in the "Salle des Conférences" of the Hôtel de Ville, at Geneva, the Tribunal assembled to listen to the opening discourse of the President, Count Sclopis, and to take up the business remaining for the consideration of the Arbitrators.

Count Sclopis, in this discourse, expressed belief that the meeting of the Tribunal indicated of itself the impression of new direction on the public policy of nations the most advanced in civilization, and the commencement of an epoch in which the spirit of moderation and the sentiment of equity were beginning to prevail over the tendency of the old routines of arbitrary violence or culpable indifference. He signified regret that the pacific views of the Congress of Paris had not been seconded by events in Europe. He congratulated the world that the statesmen who directed the destinies of Great Britain and the United States, with rare firmness of conviction and devotion to the interests of humanity, resisting all temptations of vulgar ambition, had magnanimously and courageously traversed in peace the difficulties which had divided them both before and since the conclusion of the Treaty. He quoted approvingly the opinion expressed by Mr. Gladstone, on the one hand, and by President Washington, on the other, in commendation of the policy of peace, of justice, and of honor in the conduct of nations. And he proclaimed in behalf of his colleagues, as well as of himself, the purpose of the Tribunal, acting sometimes with the large perception of statesmen, sometimes with the scrutinizing eye of judges, and always with a profound sentiment of equity and with absolute impartiality, thus to discharge its high duty of pacification as well as of justice to the two Governments.

The discourse was worthy of the occasion and of the man.

Count Frederic Sclopis of Salerano, Minister of State and Senator of the new Kingdom of Italy, has attained the ripe age of seventy-four years in the assiduous cultivation of letters, and in the discharge of the highest political and judicial functions. The countryman and the friend of Count Cavour, it was his fortune to co-operate in the task of the unification of Italy under the leadership of the House of Savoy.

This great military House, with its enterprising, ambitious, and politic instincts, second in fortune only to the Habsburgs and the Zollerns, rose in the eleventh century, on the ruins of the Burgundians, to the possession of the passes of the Valaisian, Cottian, and

Graian Alps, and of the Gallic territory on both shores of Lake Leman, and at length to the possession of extensive Italian territories, denominated Piedmont by relation to the Alps and the Apennines, the nucleus of the present Kingdom of Italy.

It needs to conceive and picture to the mind's eye the Alpine cradle of this adventurous and martial, but cultivated race of Italianized Savoisian princes, nobles, and people,—the fertile, but ravaged valleys of the Rhone, the Arve, the Albarine, the Arc, and the two Doras; the castellated heights of L'Ecluse, Montmélian, and La Brunnetta; the vine-clad hill-sides and the lofty *cols* dominated by the giant peaks of Mont Blanc and Monte Rosa; the sepulchral monuments of Haute-Combe and of Brou, and the rich plains along the Italian foot of the Alps,—in order to comprehend the growth to greatness of sovereigns such as Vittorio Emanuele, supported by such generals as Menabrea and Cialdini, and statesmen and magistrates such as Azeglio, Balbo, Sclopis, and especially Cavour.

Like his compatriot, the Marquis d'Azeglio, Count Sclopis is eminent as an author. Of his published writings, some are in French, such as "Marie Louise Gabrielle de Savoie" and "Cardinal Morone." But his most important works are in Italian; and above all, the learned "Storia della Legislazione Italiana," the last edition of which, in five volumes, is a most interesting and instructive exhibition of the successive stages of the mediæval and modern legislation of all the different States of Italy.

Such was the eminent personage who presided over

and conducted the deliberations of the Tribunal, and who represented and spoke for it on ceremonial occasions: a man of large stature and dignified presence; of the high breeding of rank, but without pretensiveness; cordial and kindly in social intercourse; the impersonation, as it were, of the intellect and the culture of Continental Europe.

MR. STÆMPFLI.

Sitting by the right hand of Count Sclopis, as next to him in precedence, not by reason of age,—for he was the youngest member of the Tribunal,—but as representing the local Government, Switzerland, was Mr. James [or, in German, Jacob] Stæmpfli: a genuine representative of democratic institutions,—sprung from the people,—the son of his own works,—clear-headed, strong-minded, firm-hearted,—somewhat positive,—not prone to talk except when talk was of the essence of things, and then briefly and to the point,—in a word, a man of the very stuff out of which to make Presidents of Federal Republics.

Mr. Stæmpfli is a German Swiss of the Canton of Berne, who has risen from the humblest to the highest condition in his country by mere force of intellect and indomitable will. Born in 1820, admitted to the Bar in 1843, he came forward at once as an advocate, and as a journalist of radical opinions, and speedily attained distinction. In 1846 we find him a conspicuous member of the Council of State, directing the finances, and laboring to organize a central military force. In 1847 he represented the Canton of Berne in the Diet, and was active in asserting the rights of the Federation against the seceding States of the Sonderbund. He served in that war as Treasurer and Paymaster-General of the Army. Displaced for a while, he resumed the practice of his profession as advocate, but soon returned to power, in 1851, as President of the National Council, where he continued to be distinguished as a close reasoner and incisive speaker, full of intelligence and of resources, supported by great energy of character. In 1856, he was elected President of the Confederation, and again in 1859, and the third time in 1862: these repeated but interrupted re-elections illustrating the Swiss Constitution, according to which the President is elected for one year only, and can not be re-elected for the next succeeding year, but is otherwise re-eligible without limitation. Events of great importance to Switzerland occurred in the years of the administration of Mr. Stæmpfli; among others, the separation of Neuchâtel from Prussia, the war in Italy, and the annexion of Savoy to France. His theory of executive action was characteristic of the man, namely, "When peril is certain, it is better to advance to meet it, rather than timidly to await its approach." In fine, *preparation* and *decision* are the distinctive traits of all the official acts of Mr. Stæmpfli.

There is one peculiarity in the political character of Mr. Stæmpfli, which belongs to him, indeed, as a Swiss, namely, definiteness and affirmativeness in the matter of international neutrality and morality. Switzerland no longer permits capitulations of foreign enlistment: they are expressly forbidden by the Federal Constitution. Her laws punish as a crime all violation by individuals of the international rights of foreign Powers. Her neutrality is active, not passive,—preventive, as well as punitive. She has no maritime relations, it is true; but, in dealing with unlawful equipments or expeditions by land, she observes rules of neutrality which are applicable, in theory and practice, equally to equipments or expeditions for naval warfare. Our own temporary act of 1838, which comprehends *vehicles* [on land] and *vessels* [on water] in the same clause of criminality, affords complete answer to those Englishmen who have superficially assumed that because Switzerland is not a maritime Power, she [or a statesman of hers] could not competently judge the case of the *Alabama* or the *Florida*. Diligence to execute the law,—vigilance to prevent its violation,—is the same in Switzerland as in Italy or Brazil, in Great Britain or the United States. And the position of Switzerland, which requires of her the *spontaneous* execution of her neutrality laws, had evident effect on the mind of Mr. Stæmpfli to produce those conclusions of his against Great Britain, which, as we shall see in the sequel, were so grossly misapprehended and so angrily resented by Sir Alexander Cockburn.

At the time when the Swiss Government invited Mr. Stæmpfli to act as Arbitrator for Switzerland under the Treaty of Washington, he had full occupation in public or private affairs as a member of the National Council and as President of the Federal

(Eidgenossische) Bank established at Berne. On receiving the respective "Counter-Cases" of the two Governments, which in effect closed the proofs on both sides, he took a characteristic step in order to be prepared for action in June.

As you sail up the Lake of Thun toward Unterseen or Interlaken, you note on the left the precipitous wooded mountain-side of Beatenberg. Here, high up in a rural hamlet, hidden among the trees, with the beautiful lakes of Thun and Brienz at his feet, and the magnificent spectacle of the Oberland, terminating at the remoter Berner Alps,—in those balmy Alpine days when spring is passing into summer, and all earth is a paradise of verdure and of animation,—here Mr. Stæmpfli secluded himself from the social distractions and cares of business at Berne, and dedicated himself to the mastery of the "*Alabama* Claims.*"* In such a blessed retreat even law-books might lose their dullness, and diplomatic correspondence, depositions, and legal pleadings be invested with the charmed reflection of the matchless scenery of lakes, fields, hamlets, cities, mountains, and rivers, glittering in the sun, and resting in the horizon at the snow-crowned heights of the Jungfrau.

And so it seems to have been. For good St. Beatus blessed the mountain labors of Mr. Stæmpfli, and he came to Geneva in due time with full abstracts of evidence and elaborately written opinions on the main questions at issue before the Tribunal, to the apparent surprise of Sir Alexander Cockburn, who, confidently relying on the rupture of the Arbitration, as he himself avowed, had not yet begun to examine the cause, and seemed to suppose that every body else ought to be as neglectfully ignorant of it as himself: which sentiment betrayed itself on various occasions in the sittings of the Tribunal.

VISCOUNT OF ITAJUBÁ.

On the left of Count Sclopis sat the Arbitrator named by the Emperor of Brazil, the Viscount of Itajubá.

The people of the United States do not seem to be generally aware how much of high cultivation, especially [but not exclusively] in the departments of diplomacy and jurisprudence, exists in those countries of America which were colonized by Spain and Portugal. Nevertheless, on careful consideration of the sterling merits of such historical writers as the Mexican Lucas Alaman,—such authors of international jurisprudence as the Chilean Bello, the Argentine Calvo, or the Peruvian Pando,—such writers of belles-lettres, of travels, or of statistics, as the Colombians Samper and Perez,—such poets as the Brazilian Magalhaens, —such codes of municipal law as those of the States of Cundinamarca and of Mexico or of the Argentine Confederation, and of other Republics of Spanish America,—we should be compelled to admit that literature and science are not confined to our part of the New World.

And, among all these new Powers of America, there is not one more deserving of respect,—Empire and not Republic though it be,—than Brazil, in view of the magnitude of its territory, the greatness of its resources, its military strength and successes, its enlightened and reforming chief ruler, the substantial liberality of its political institutions, and the unbroken domestic tranquillity of its independent life, so strikingly in contrast with the revolutionary agitations of most of the Spanish-American Republics.

Marcos Antonio d'Araujo belongs to that numerous body of jurists and statesmen, the natural growth of parliamentary institutions based on popular election, who do honor at the present time to Brazil. He filled in early life the chair of Professor of Jurisprudence in the University of Pernambuco. His first diplomatic appointment was that of Consul-General of Brazil in the Hanse Towns, with residence at Hamburg. After that he held successively the offices of Minister or Envoy at Hanover, at Copenhagen, at Berlin, and finally at Paris. At the time of his appointment as Arbitrator he was Envoy Extraordinary and Minister Plenipotentiary of Brazil in France, by the title of Baron d'Itajubá, and he was made a Viscount during the progress of the Arbitration.

With exception, therefore, of the judicial studies and occupations of his youth, the Viscount of Itajubá is a diplomatist, having passed nearly forty years of his life in the discharge of diplomatic functions in different countries of Europe. He possesses all the qualities of his career and station, namely, courteous and attractive manners, intelligence disciplined by long experience of men and affairs, instinctive appreciation of principles and facts, and the ready expression of thought in apt language, but without the tendency to run into the path of debate or exposition, which appeared in the acts of some of his colleagues of the Tribunal of Arbitration.

In comparing Mr. Stæmpfli, with his deep-brown complexion, his piercing dark eyes, his jet black hair, his quick but suppressed manner, and the Viscount of Itajubá, with his fair complexion and his air of gentleness and affability, one, having no previous knowledge of their respective origins, would certainly attribute that of the former to tropical and passionate America, and that of the latter to temperate and calm-blooded Europe.

SIR ALEXANDER COCKBURN.

On the extremes of the Board, Mr. Adams to the right and Sir Alexander Cockburn to the left, sat the American and British members of the Tribunal.

Sir Alexander Cockburn represents a family of some distinction, the Cockburns of Langton. His father was British Minister in Colombia, and one of his uncles was that Admiral Sir George Cockburn, whose service in American waters during our last war with Great Britain has left some unpleasant traces or memories in the United States. His mother seems to have been a French lady, being described by Burke as "Yolande, dau. of Viscomte de Vignier of St. Domingo." He was born in 1802, called to the bar in 1829, became distinguished as a barrister, entered Parliament, and, after passing through the routine offices of Solicitor and Attorney General, was made Chief Justice of the Court of Common Pleas in 1856, and of the Queen's Bench in 1859, which place he still fills.

He presided for sixteen years in the common-law courts of England without being raised to the peerage. It is unnecessary to speculate on the reasons for this unusual, if not unprecedented fact.

His political career dates from his zealous defense of Lord Palmerston in the affair of the notorious David Pacifico. This person was an adventurer of doubtful nationality and of bad character, in whose behalf the navy of Great Britain, under Lord Palmerston's direction, seized the Piræus, captured Greek merchant-vessels, and threatened Athens. The ground of claim was alleged destruction of property by a mob. Pacifico claimed, according to the official statement of the case by the British Government, £4916 on account of furniture and other personal effects, which he originally stated at only 5000 francs, and £26,618 16$s.$ 8$d.$ on account of papers. It is very doubtful whether the claim was a proper subject of international reclamation. But, after a three months' blockade, Greece submitted to pay £5000, of which £4720 was either falsehood or consequential damages; and afterward, on examination of the case in Lisbon, a commission awarded the petty sum of £150 in full satisfaction of the pretended loss of £26,618, induced perhaps by political reasons rather than by conviction of any rights of Pacifico.

The conduct of Lord Palmerston and the British Government in this affair nearly involved Great Britain in a war with France and Russia. The French Embassador retired from London to Paris for the purpose of personal communication on the subject with his Government. Count Nesselrode on behalf of Russia remonstrated in a dispatch, which the London *Times* characterized as reproachful, irrefutable, and just, and as profoundly affecting the peace of Europe and the dignity of Great Britain. The united voice of Europe and America has condemned the conduct of Great Britain in this affair. The House of Lords closed an historic debate by a vote of censure of the Government. In the Commons, the last words of Sir Robert Peel were raised in protest against this outrage on the rights of other nations; the morning dawned on a protracted session of the House before he recorded his vote of condemnation; in the afternoon of the same day he met with the accident which closed his honorable life. Mr. Gladstone in the same debate said that the claim was "on the very face of it an outrageous fraud and falsehood;" that "it was mere falsehood and imposture," and that "a greater iniquity had rarely been transacted under the face of the sun."

Sir Alexander Cockburn was then without parliamentary distinction or political advancement. With the devotion of a Dalgetty, he placed his lance at the service of a chief, regardless of the merits of the cause. He was soon rewarded for his services by appointment to the office of Solicitor-General, from which he was promoted step by step, with unexampled celerity, to his present position.

Since he became the head of the Queen's Bench he has occasionally appeared in the field of letters on questions connected with municipal or public law, but not in a way to invite respect at home, or attention beyond the limits of Great Britain.

A few years ago he published a monogram on the subject of nationality, in which he reproduced in an abridged form [but quite incorrectly, as the remarks of a most competent judge, Mr. Beach Lawrence, on *droit d'aubaine*, tend to show] the matter contained in the report of a commission appointed by the Government to inquire into and report upon the laws of naturalization and allegiance in England.

Again, when it was proposed to arraign Nelson and Brand as criminals in England for acts committed in Jamaica under proclamation of martial law, Sir Alexander Cockburn delivered a voluminous charge to the grand jury, which he afterward published with additions and notes, notwithstanding the partiality and the urgency of which, the grand jury refused to find a bill; and it must be confessed that, as a charge, it was passionate, vague, declamatory, and confused; and as an exposition of law, it is valueless when compared with the treatises of Mr. Finlason, in England, and of Mr. Whiting, in America, on the same subject.

This charge, and some proceedings by which it was followed, provoked much criticism. Mr. Gathorne Hardy, for instance, called attention to the fact that the Chief Justice "vacillated," that he "went from one side to another," so as to render it doubtful what his opinions really were; and Mr.

Hardy, as well as Mr. Mill, who spoke on the other side of the general question, said that the charge was "not law," and was "without legal authority." Mr. Finlason, a most competent authority, said that, "although the charge dealt so largely in denunciation," it was "utterly indeterminate and indecisive;" that "it avowed a state of entire doubt;" that, though "there was much denunciation of law laid down [by others], there was no positive declaration of law laid down by the Chief Justice." The same writer also points out grave mistakes of history as well as errors of law in this charge. Thus, the Chief Justice assumes, as a cardinal thought, that *martial law* and *military law* are one and the same thing: a mistake, which implies extraordinary confusion of mind, forgetfulness of his own official opinions in the incidents of the rebellion in Ceylon, and ignorance of the most commonplace events of English history, for instance, as detailed in Hallam and Macaulay.

I allude to these criticisms for the reason that, as will appear in the sequel, the same singular intellectual traits and moral characteristics of the Chief Justice, which became conspicuous at Geneva, had shown themselves on the Queen's Bench, and had attracted the notice of his fellow-countrymen.

I refer to this charge for another cause. It is difficult for many reasons to measure the exact *personal* value of ordinary legal opinions delivered, in the course of adjudication, by any judge of the Queen's Bench. All such difficulties cease when he goes out of his way to deliver a demonstrative charge to a grand jury on one of the semi-political questions of the day, and especially when such charge is carefully revised for the Press, with additions and annotations by himself. Then we have the most satisfactory means of estimating the mental character of that judge. And such is the case here, to the effect of lowering greatly our estimation of the Chief Justice.

A later incident in his judicial career also throws some light on his character, and deserves notice in this connection.

When it was proposed to commence proceedings against Governor Eyre, growing out of what had been done in Jamaica under the same proclamation, Mr. Justice Blackburn delivered a charge to the grand jury, in the course of which he said: "As to the judges of my own court, the Lord Chief Justice, my brother Mellor, my brother Lush, and my brother Hannen, . . . yesterday I stated to them the effect of what I am now stating to you, and they all approved of it, and authorized me to say,—of course, not relieving me from my responsibility, or absolutely binding them, for of course they have not considered it so thoroughly and judicially as I have been obliged to do,—still they authorize me to say they agree in my view of the law, and thought it right." A week later, when the case had been entirely disposed of, the Chief Justice, while sitting on the Bench, denied, with unseemly warmth of language and manner, that he had assented to the law as laid down by Mr. Justice Blackburn; but explained the alleged difference of opinion in such obscure language as to render it scarcely intelligible. Mr. Justice Blackburn replied, reiterating in temperate language his statement that the Chief Justice had expressly assented to the legal doctrine of the charge, and his colleagues, Justices Mellor, Lush, and Hannen, gave no support to the denial made by the Chief Justice.

The qualities of character exhibited in this incident were the occasion at the time of unfavorable commentary on the part of the British Press and public.

Sir Alexander Cockburn had seemed, on superficial view, a fit person to take part in the important duties committed to the Tribunal of Arbitration. He carried thither the prestige of judicial rank, as the head of one of the most venerable courts of Europe. And he was thorough master of the language in which the discussions of the Tribunal were conducted.

But, unfortunately, it would seem that neither the original constitution of his mind, nor the studies, pursuits, or habits of his life, had fitted him for calm, impartial, judicial examination of great questions of public law. The same traits of confused thought, equivocation in matters of law, tendency to declamatory denunciation of adversary opinions, which provoked and justified the criticisms of Mr. Finlason, Mr. Gathorne Hardy, and others, and which prompted conflict with Mr. Justice Blackburn, reappeared in more vivid colors at Geneva.

Of the offensive singularities of his *deportment* as

Arbitrator, we shall have but too much necessity to speak in describing the acts of the Tribunal.

MR. CHARLES FRANCIS ADAMS.

In the American Arbitrator, Mr. Charles Francis Adams, the Tribunal had a member worthy of the companionship of Count Frederic Sclopis.

In the United States, persons have been found so foolish as to reproach Mr. Adams because of the historical eminence of his father and of his grandfather, and even because of the intelligence and cultivation of his sons: as if it were a crime in a Republic for a father to have a good son, or a son a good father, or to live in the holy atmosphere of a succession of wise and virtuous mothers.

Besides, if it be meritorious to rise to distinction from lowliness and poverty, it is not less so to resist and overcome the obstacles to personal distinction created by parental station or wealth. In this, which is the only correct view of the subject, all men are self-made. The attributes of Mr. Charles Francis Adams are his own: distinguished parliamentary career in the Legislature of the State of Massachusetts and in the Congress of the United States,—literary merits of a high order as displayed in his "Life and Writings of John Adams,"—able diplomatic representation of his Government in Great Britain during the whole dark period of our Civil War. He possessed qualities, acquirements, and experience, general and special, which seemed to invite his appointment as American Arbitrator; and in the discharge of the duties of the office he did honor to the Tribunal and to the United States.

The deportment of Mr. Adams as a member of the Tribunal was unexceptionably dignified, manly, courteous, even when compelled on more than one occasion to notice rude acts or words of Sir Alexander Cockburn. While the conduct of the latter was too frequently on the comparatively low plane of the *nisi prius* attorney of a party before a court, the conduct of the former was uniformly on the higher one of a member of the court and a judge. Hence, in the same degree that the personal influence of Mr. Adams, by reason of his recognized impartiality and integrity, was beneficial to the United States, on the other hand, the influence of Sir Alexander Cockburn, by reason of his petulant irritability and unjudicial partisanship of action, was unfavorable to Great Britain.

Such, then, were the Arbitrators representing the five Governments.

SECRETARY OF THE TRIBUNAL.

Their Secretary, Mr. Alexandre Favrot, was a gentlemanly person of literary attainments and profession, actually residing in Berne, but born in the French-speaking Canton of Neuchâtel, who had become perfectly acquainted with the English language by a sojourn of several years in England.

AGENTS AND COUNSEL.

The Agents of the two Governments, Lord Tenterden and Mr. Bancroft Davis, were peculiarly qualified for the places they filled, both of them having served in similar capacities in the foreign Department of their respective Governments, and both having assisted in the negotiation of the Treaty of Washington. Their friendly personal relations were advantageous in facilitating the movement of business before the Arbitration.

Mr. Bancroft Davis deserves particular mention. Englishmen may criticise the American "Case," the labor of preparing which devolved chiefly on him; but its indisputable merit should draw to him the applause of every American. His literary accomplishments, his previous diplomatic experience, his knowledge of men and things in Europe, and his devoted and untiring attention to the public interests, were singularly useful to the United States.

Of the persons or qualities of the Counsel of the United States, Mr. Morrison R. Waite, Mr. William M. Evarts, and the writer of this exposition, it would be unbecoming, as it is quite superfluous, here to speak.

In this relation, however, it is proper to call attention to two facts or incidents of national interest or concernment.

In the first place, to the honor of the President of the United States be it said, in the selection of Counsel by him, as for instance in the invitation to Mr. B. R. Curtis, considerations of *party* were not allowed to exert controlling authority.

Secondly, the Counsel themselves emulated the catholic spirit of the President in subordinating all personal considerations to the single object of winning a great cause, the greatest ever committed to the charge of members of the Bar, and pending in the highest court ever organized, namely, the suit of the United States against Great Britain before the Tribunal of Arbitration. Although diverse in their habits of mind, and in their lines of experience and action, they acted as a unit in the determination of advice to be given from time to time to the Government or its Agent;—in the preparation of the printed Argument required by the Treaty, a document of five hundred pages, to be signed by them jointly;—and in the subsequent preparation of a number of joint or separate Arguments in compliance with the requirements of the Arbitrators. We may appeal to those Arguments as the tangible proof, at any rate, of our concurrent and united dedication, during nine months of continuous and solicitous thought or labor, to the discharge of our duty to our Government and our country, as Counsel under the Treaty of Washington.

Sir Roundell Palmer alone appeared before the Tribunal as *eo nomine* Counsel of Great Britain; but Mr. Mountague Bernard, elevated to the office of a law-member of the Queen's Council, sat by his side at the Counsels' table, and also Mr. Cohen. The hand of the latter was apparent in the estimates and exhibits presented to the Tribunal to guide them in the determination of the damages to be awarded to the United States.

The recent promotion of Sir Roundell Palmer to the pre-eminent post of Lord Chancellor, by the title of Lord Selborne, is the appropriate consummation of a professional and parliamentary career of distinguished ability and of unstained honor. In conducting the deliberations of the House of Lords; in presiding over the High Court of Chancery; in participating in the affairs of the Cabinet; in guiding the conscience of the Queen through the embarrassments which now beset the English Church, we may be sure that Lord Selborne will join to the high authority of a skillful debater and a learned jurist the still higher authority of a sincerely conscientious statesman, so as to add incontestable force to Mr. Gladstone's Ministry. And all that authority, we may confidently assume, will be used in the promotion or maintenance of amicable relations between Great Britain and the United States.

This account of the *personnel* of the Arbitration would be imperfect without mention of the younger but estimable persons who constituted the staff of the formal representatives of the two Governments, namely: on the part of the United States, Mr. C. C. Beaman, as solicitor, and Messrs. Brooks Adams, John Davis, F. W. Hackett, W. F. Pedrick, and Edward T. Waite, as secretaries; and on the part of Great Britain, in the latter capacity or as translators, Messrs. Sanderson, Markheim, Villiers, Langley, and Hamilton. If the labors of these gentlemen were less conspicuous than those of the Agents and Counsel, they were scarcely less indispensable; and they all deserve a place in the history of the Arbitration.

A single observation will close up these personal

sketches, and bring us to the consideration of the ulterior proceedings of the Tribunal.

Occasionally, but not frequently, at the present day, we hear in the United States ungracious suggestions touching the personal deportment of Englishmen. No such observations, it is certain, are justified by any experience of the city of Washington. The eminent persons, who, in the present generation, have represented the British Government here, whether in permanent or special missions, such as Sir Richard Packenham, Lord Napier, Lord Lyons, Sir Frederick Bruce, and Sir Edward Thornton, of the former class, and Lord Ashburton, the Earl of Elgin, Earl De Grey, Sir Stafford Northcote, Mr. Mountague Bernard, Sir John A. Macdonald, and Lord Tenterden, of the latter class, with the younger persons of their respective suites, and so many others who have visited this city, were unmistakably and with good cause popular with the Americans. Indeed, it is rather in Continental Europe, and especially in France, and by no means in the United States, that overbearingness or uncourteous deportment toward others is regarded as a trait of Englishmen.

And it is agreeable to remember that, of the ten Englishmen with whom we of the United States came in daily contact at Geneva, and sometimes in circumstances of contentious attitude of a nature to produce coolness at least, all but one were uniformly and unexceptionably courteous in act and manner,—and that one Chief Justice of the Queen's Bench.

Is a holder of the office of Chief Justice emancipated from all social bonds? It is not so with Chief Justices in America; nor was it so in former days in Great Britain, according to my recollection of the great judges, the Eldons, the Tenterdens, and the Stowells, who then presided over the administration of the common law, and of the equity and admiralty jurisprudence of England. Has the human race there degenerated? I think not: no possible judicial tenure of office could transform or deform a Roundell Palmer into an Alexander Cockburn.

EFFORTS OF THE BRITISH GOVERNMENT TO OBTAIN REARGUMENT.

The Tribunal and the persons attending it are now before us, and we resume its proceedings at the point where we left them, namely, the session of the 27th of June, at the close of the address of Count Sclopis.

The "Argument," filed in behalf of the United States on the 15th of June, was prepared and delivered in strict conformity with the stipulations of the Treaty. It was, in effect, the closing argument on the whole case, consisting of an abridged view of the facts on both sides as presented in their "Cases" and "Counter-Cases," with appropriate discussion of the questions of law which the claims of the United States involved. We followed the ordinary routine of judicial controversy, and the course of common-sense and of necessity, in giving a complete *résumé* of our Case in the final "Argument," as contemplated and prescribed by the Treaty.

The "Case" and "Counter-Case" of each side had

sufficiently indicated the scope of inquiry or debate, and defined its limits. Within those limits all pertinent law, history, and reason lay at the command of the Counsel of the United States, as of those of Great Britain. If we, the Counsel of the United States, had neglected at the proper time to avail ourselves of the great stores of knowledge and of reason accessible to us, we could not expect to supply the deficiencies of our "Argument" by filing a new one as the means of response to, and commentary on, the British "Argument." Such procedure was not authorized,—it was plainly forbidden,—by the Treaty.

It avails nothing to say that the course prescribed by the Treaty is *unusual:* such was the will of the two Governments. Doubtless they had good reasons, and among them, perhaps, was the very purpose of not having final "Arguments,"—that is, the *third* argument in effect on both sides,—consist of a mere debate of reply and rejoinder betwixt Counsel.

Great Britain had no cause or excuse for misapprehension in this respect, although both Government and Counsel had, it is true, fallen into the careless way of speaking of the "Summary" to be filed on the 15th of June. Nay, the paper filed by Great Britain is expressly entitled "Argument *or Summary.*" If *argument* and *summary* are synonymous terms, then it is tautology and bad taste to employ them both to designate the same document. If they mean different things, then it is misleading to employ the term summary at all; for *summary* is not the language nor the sense of the Treaty. The Treaty requires each Agent to deliver "a written or printed argument showing the points and referring to the evidence upon which his Government relies." Do these words imply a weak or imperfect argument? Do they define the number of pages to be occupied? Do they require either of the parties to leave out his strong points? Of course not. And if the Treaty said "summary,"—which it does not,—who shall say what is a fit *summary* of some twenty volumes of evidence and of legal discussions, such as the two "Cases" and "Counter-Cases" comprehend? The United States had the right to judge for themselves what exhibition of "points" and what "evidence" to submit to the Arbitrators.

The British Government must have been *dissatisfied* with its own argument. That is clear, and is the only sufficient explanation of the earnest and persistent efforts of Sir Roundell Palmer to obtain permission to reargue the cause. There was no misapprehension on the part of the British Government as to the more or less fullness of argumentation admissible in the so-called "Argument;" for there is notable similitude in this respect on both sides in the introductory language of the final "Arguments" of the two Governments. We believed at the time, and all the subsequent occurrences tended to prove, that as the British Government had underestimated the force of our cause until the "Case" came into their hands, so they did not appreciate the amplitude of our law and our evidence until they read our "Argument."

And strange, almost incredible, though it be, the

British Government would seem to have supposed that the United States were to discuss and confute the British "Counter-Case" in the American "Counter-Case;" that is, to make reply to an elaborate argument on the law and the facts [for such is the British "Counter-Case"] without seeing it or possessing any knowledge of its contents. Manifestly, no complete and systematic final "Argument" on the part of the United States was possible without previous thoughtful knowledge of the British "Counter-Case." And yet Sir Roundell Palmer, in expressing desire to *answer* our "Argument," reasoned expressly on the implication that it ought to have been "*a mere complement of previous documents.*" No such idea certainly is conveyed by the Treaty; and the implication is contrary to reason and the very nature of things.

Sir Roundell Palmer entered on the question the moment it became reasonably certain that the Arbitration would proceed. On the 29th of June he proposed to us, informally, to arrange for reargument of the cause, he to have until the end of the first week of August to prepare his Argument, and we to the end of August to prepare a reply. The effect of this would be a suspension of the sittings for more than ten weeks, and a prolongation to that extent [and perhaps much more] of the absence of the American Arbitrator, Agent, and Counsel from their country. In other respects the proposition involved much inequality; for it would have given to the British Counsel *nearly six weeks* at his own home in London, with books, assistants, translators, and printing-offices at his command,—in a word, the whole force of the British Government at his back, in which to write and print his Argument; while it would have afforded to the American Counsel *less than four weeks* for the same task, in which to prepare and print our Argument in both languages, with no libraries at hand, no translators, no printers, thrown wholly on our personal resources away from home in the heart of Europe.

The Counsel of the United States desired no reargument of the cause. We found nothing in the British Argument which we had not anticipated and disposed of to our own satisfaction. Not that we feared reargument: on the contrary, we felt such complete confidence in our rights as to be sure not to lose, and to hope rather to gain, by further discussion. Hence we did not desire nor seek reargument, although perfectly ready for it if called upon in conformity with the Treaty. Our objections were to the delay and to the departure from the conditions of the Treaty.

According to the explicit language of the Treaty, " the decision of the Tribunal shall, if possible, be made within three months from the close of the arguments on both sides;" and the prescribed day "for the close of the arguments on both sides" is the 15th of June. Suppose that, by agreement of the two Governments,—it could not be done by Counsel without consent of their Governments,—"the close of the arguments" had been postponed to the 31st of August, as proposed by Sir Roundell Palmer. In that event the Arbitrators could not in reason or decency have commenced their deliberations until the 1st of September; they might well have taken, as they did in fact take, three months to complete their deliberations; and thus the Arbitrators and the *American* Counsel [but not the English] would have been detained at Geneva until the 1st of December, and therefore would not have been able to reach their homes until January.

But the reargument proposed by Sir Roundell Palmer was contrary to the Treaty, which in express terms closes the rights of the two Governments as to hearing, and admits further discussion on their part only at the requisition of the Arbitrators, "if they desire further elucidation in regard to any point." [Art. V.] Which manifestly intends, not reargument of the cause, but solution of any doubt, which, after the completion of the arguments, may occur to the Tribunal. No consent of Counsel could annul the stipulations of the Treaty.

Of course, for reasons of right as well as expediency, we declined to accede to the proposition of Sir Roundell Palmer.

Nevertheless, at the meeting of the 27th, immediately after the conclusion of Count Sclopis's discourse, Lord Tenterden presented a motion on the part of Sir Roundell Palmer for leave to file a written argument in answer to the Argument of the United States delivered on the 15th, and requesting adjournment for that purpose until August. Sir Roundell Palmer read a brief of the points he desired to argue, which covered in effect all the points of the American "Case" and "Argument,"—that is to say, it implied a complete reargument of the whole cause. It amounted to assuming or admitting that no sufficient or proper defense had yet been made by the British Government.

We, in behalf of the United States, proceeded to prepare a reply to this motion. We took it up point by point, and showed by citation of pages that every one of the proposed points had been largely and amply discussed already by Great Britain in her "Case," "Counter-Case," and "Argument;" that nothing new could be said on these points; and that, in fact, the very object proposed was to reiterate arguments already adduced, but to do it in the inadmissible form of mere criticism of the American Argument. And we cited the Treaty to show that the discussion proposed was contrary to the explicit contract of the two Governments.

Meanwhile the Tribunal proceeded to decide, on suggestion of Mr. Adams, that the proposed argument was inadmissible, and that Counsel had no right to address the Tribunal unless required by it so to do for the elucidation of any point under the 5th article of the Treaty.

At the next meeting of the Tribunal, on the 28th, Sir Alexander Cockburn presented a list of eight points covering in effect the points of the rejected motion of Sir Roundell Palmer, and moved that the Tribunal require of the Counsel of the two Governments written or printed arguments on the said points;

but the Tribunal decided not at present to require such arguments.

Whether the motion of Sir Alexander Cockburn was prompted by Sir Roundell Palmer, in order to afford to the latter the desired opportunity to criticise the American "Argument,"—or whether it was a spontaneous one arising from the former's not having studied the case, and his consequent ignorance of the fact that most of the questions proposed had already been amply and sufficiently discussed by both Governments,—does not distinctly appear. Probably both motives co-operated to induce the motion. Subsequent incidents throw some light on this point. Meanwhile it was plain to infer from the observations of the other Arbitrators, and from their decision, that they were better informed on the subject than Sir Alexander Cockburn.

RULES CONCERNING THE CONFERENCES OF THE TRIBUNAL.

The Tribunal next decided that the Agents should attend all the discussions and deliberations of the Conferences, accompanied by the Counsel, except in case where the Tribunal should think it advisable to conduct their discussions and deliberations with closed doors. The practical effect of this resolution, when connected with a resolution adopted at a subsequent meeting in regard to the course of proceeding, was to enable and require the Agents and Counsel to assist at the judicial consultations of the Tribunal: it being understood, of course, that none others should be present save the representatives of the two Governments.

The Tribunal then authorized publicity to be given to its declaration and to the declarations of the two Governments, relative to the national claims of the United States: after which it adjourned to the 15th of July.

Heretofore, either by intimation to the Secretary, and to the Agents and Counsel, or by formal resolution, the Tribunal had signified its desire that the proceedings should not be committed to publicity, unless by the will of the respective Governments. Of course, reporters for the Press, and other persons not officially connected with the Arbitration, were excluded from the sittings of the Tribunal. This reserve or secrecy of proceeding was inconvenient to the many respectable representatives of the Press of London and New York, persons of consideration, who had come to Geneva for the purpose of satisfying the public curiosity of the United States and of England regarding the acts of the Tribunal; but was dictated, it would seem, rather by considerations of delicacy toward the two Governments, than by any reluctance on the part of the Arbitrators to have their action made known day by day to the world. It was a tribunal of peculiar constitution and character; its members were responsible in some sense each to his own Government, and also to the opinion, at least, of the litigant Governments; its proceedings were not purely judicial, but in a certain degree diplomatic; and a large part of the proceedings were in the nature not so much of action, as of judicial consultation, which it might well seem unfit to communicate to the general public as they occurred, although perfectly fit to be thus communicated to the respective Governments.

The Tribunal reassembled on the 15th of July. Down to this time all the proceedings of the Arbitrators were in their nature public acts, or they have been made public through the respective Governments. All such acts were recorded in the protocols.

Hereafter, we shall have, in addition to the acts of the Tribunal recorded in protocols, a series of provisional opinions, which were also printed and distributed [or should have been] according to express order of the Tribunal. These opinions of the Arbitrators, as well as their official acts, have already been made public by both Governments.

But, incidentally to such acts and opinions, there was much oral debate from time to time at the successive Conferences of the Tribunal. At these debates, the Agents and Counsel of both Governments were required to assist, by resolution of the Tribunal. Assisting, we necessarily heard what was said by the respective Arbitrators. We were expected to hear, it is presumable, and also to understand: otherwise, why required to attend?

Are these debates, which occurred in the presence of so many persons, Agents, Counsel, and others, to be regarded as confidential and unfit to be disclosed now? Forget them, we can not, even if copious notes of the most important debates did not exist to aid and correct mere memory. Is it, then, improper to speak of them? I think not. I conceive that any of us, who possess knowledge of those debates, have perfect right to refer to them on all fit occasions.

I propose, however, on the present occasion, to exercise this right sparingly, and that only in two relations, namely, first, very briefly, where such reference involves mere formality, and is almost inseparable from acts recorded in the protocols; and, secondly, with a little more fullness at the close, and with some retrospection, for the purpose of explaining the final act of the British Arbitrator.

DISCUSSIONS OF THE TRIBUNAL.

At the meeting of the 15th, discussion arose immediately as to the method and order of proceeding to be adopted in the consideration of the subjects referred to the Tribunal.

Mr. Stæmpfli then suggested that in his opinion the proper course was to take up the case of some vessel, as expressly required by the Treaty, and consider whether on that vessel Great Britain was responsible to the United States. He had directed his own inquiries in this way, and in this way had arrived at satisfactory conclusions. His plan had been to select a vessel,—to abstract the facts proved regarding her,—and then to apply to the facts the special rules of the Treaty.

Debate on this proposition ensued between Sir Alexander Cockburn, on the one hand, and the rest of the Arbitrators on the other hand; the former desiring to have preliminary consideration of "principles," that is, of abstract questions of law, and the latter insisting that the true and logical course was that of the Treaty, namely, to take up a case, to examine the facts, and to discuss and apply the law to the facts thus ascertained, as proposed by Mr. Stæmpfli.

Finally it was concluded, on the proposition of Count Sclopis, to follow substantially the programme of Mr. Stæmpfli, that is, to take up the inculpated vessels, *seriatim*, each Arbitrator to express an opinion in writing thereon, of such tenor as he should see fit, but these opinions to be *provisional* only for the present, and not to conclude the Arbitrator, or to prevent his modifying such opinion, on arriving at the point of participation in the final decision of the Tribunal.

On the 16th, consideration of the programme of Mr. Stæmpfli was resumed. It consisted of the following heads, which deserve to be set forth here, in order to show how thoroughly the subject had been examined and digested by Mr. Stæmpfli.

" (A.) Indications générales :
    1. Question à decider.
    2. Délimitation des faits.
    3. Principes généraux.
" (B.) Décision relative à chacun des croiseurs.
    Observations préliminaires :
    1. Le Sumter.
      (*a*) Faits.
      (*b*) Considérants.
      (*c*) Jugement."

[Follow the names of the other vessels, with similar sub-division of heads of inquiry.]

" (C.) Détermination du Tribunal d'adjuger une somme en bloc.

" (D.) Examen des éléments pour fixer une somme en bloc.

" (E.) Conclusion et adjudication définitive d'une somme en bloc."

The completeness and exactness of this programme are self-evident; and by these qualities it really imposed itself on the Tribunal, in spite of all objection, and of occasional temporary departures into other lines of thought. There will be occasion hereafter to remark on the precision and concision of the opinions of Mr. Stæmpfli.

SIR ALEXANDER COCKBURN'S CALL FOR REARGUMENT.

Sir Alexander Cockburn then renewed his proposition for a preliminary argument by Counsel, setting forth analytically the various objects of inquiry involved in the claims of the United States, and concluding as follows:

"That, looking to the difficulty of these questions, and the conflict of opinion which has arisen among distinguished jurists on the present contest, as well as to their vast importance in the decision of the Tribunal on the matters in dispute, it is the duty, as it must be presumed to be the wish, of the Arbitrators, in the interests of justice, to obtain all the assistance in their power to enable them to arrive at a just and correct conclusion. That they ought, therefore, to call for the assistance of the eminent counsel who are in attendance on the Tribunal to assist them with their reasoning and learning, so that arguments scattered over a mass of documents may be presented in a concentrated and appreciable form, and the Tribunal may thus have the advantage of all the light which can be thrown on so intricate and difficult a matter, and that its proceedings may hereafter appear to the world to have been characterized by the patience, the deliberation, and anxious desire for information on all the points involved in its decision, without which it is impossible that justice can be duly or satisfactorily done."

"To obtain all the *assistance* in their power to en-

able them to arrive at a just and correct conclusion,"
—"to call for the *assistance* of the eminent counsel who are in attendance on the Tribunal to *assist* them with their reasoning and learning."

Analyzing the proposition, and omitting the introductory and concluding phrases of more or less irrelevant and diffuse appeal to extraneous considerations, the essence of the proposition is to call on Counsel to assist the Tribunal, "so that arguments scattered over a mass of documents may be presented in a concentrated and appreciable form."

Now, passing over the looseness and inaccuracy of expression in this statement, it plainly is incorrect in substance. The considerations of law or fact necessary for the instruction of the Tribunal are *not* "scattered over a mass of documents;" they *are* "presented in a concentrated ... form" [we do not say *appreciable*, because that is not a quality intelligible as applied to *form*] in the three arguments of each of the Governments,—that is to say, "Cases," "Counter-Cases," and "Arguments." The proposition betrays singular confusion of mind on the part of a *nisi prius* lawyer and judge. The subjects or elements of argument are, it is true, "scattered over a mass of documents;" but it is quite absurd to apply this phrase to the Arguments themselves, in which the two Governments had each labored, we may suppose, to exhibit their views of the law and the facts in a manner to be readily comprehended and appreciated by the Tribunal. In the Arguments proper, filed on the 15th of June, each Agent had, as the Treaty requires, delivered "to each of the said Arbitrators and to the Agent of the other party a written or printed argument showing the points and referring to the evidence on which his Government relies." These "Arguments" were freshly in the possession of the Arbitrators. To call on Counsel, *for the reason assigned*, to reargue the matters therein argued, was just as unreasonable as it would be for a judge presiding at a hearing in common law, equity, or admiralty, to call on the counsel, who have just finished their arguments, to do something for the "assistance" of the Court,—it would be difficult to see what,—to the end "that arguments scattered over a mass of documents may be presented in a concentrated and appreciable form." And if in this case such arguments had been filed in print, it would be natural for counsel to say that they had just done the thing required of them, as the Court would perceive if it would please to read those arguments: which, in the present case, it would seem, Sir Alexander had neglected to do; and, instead of doing it, he had got bewildered by plunging unpreparedly into the "mass of documents" filed by the two Governments.

After discussion, the Tribunal decided to proceed with the case of the *Florida*, according to the programme of Mr. Stæmpfli, that is, in effect, overruling the motion of Sir Alexander Cockburn.

The Tribunal, it would seem, could not perceive the advantage of discussing speculative general questions, as in a moot court; and, more especially, questions of law, which had already been discussed abun-

H

dantly in the appropriate place and time, that is, in the successive Cases and Arguments of the two Governments.

CASE OF THE "FLORIDA" DECIDED.

The Arbitrators then met on the 17th, and proceeded to take up the case of the *Florida*.

On motion of Sir Alexander Cockburn, it was ordered by the Tribunal that the provisional opinions or statements to be read by the Arbitrators should be printed, and distributed to the Arbitrators and to the Agents and Counsel of the two Governments.

Mr. Stæmpfli's opinion or statement had been read already, and was in print.

After some incidental discussion among the Arbitrators, Sir A. Cockburn began the reading of his opinion on the case of the *Florida*.

The Tribunal met again on the 19th, and Sir Alexander Cockburn proceeded to read another portion of his opinion in the case of the *Florida*.

Then, after some debate, caused by irregularities of speech or conduct on the part of Sir Alexander, Mr. Adams proceeded to read the commencement of his opinion in the matter of the *Florida*.

On the 22d, the case of the *Florida* was concluded. Sir Alexander Cockburn and Mr. Adams completed the reading of their opinions, and the Baron d'Itajubá and Count Sclopis both read theirs. The result was to convict Great Britain of culpable want of due diligence in the matter of the *Florida* by the concurrent provisional opinions of four of the Arbitrators, with a dissenting opinion from the British Arbitrator.

The *Florida*, it will be remembered, was a steam gun-boat, built at Liverpool by Miller & Sons, on contract with the Confederate agent Bullock, for the warlike use of the Confederates. Miller & Sons falsely pretended that she was being built for the Italian Government by arrangement with Messrs. Thomas & Brothers of Liverpool and Palermo, one of whom expressly and fraudulently confirmed the false representation of Miller & Sons. The British Government, although repeatedly warned of the *illegal* character of this vessel by the diplomatic and consular authorities of the United States, shut its eyes to the transparent falsehood and fraud of Miller & Sons and of Thomas, and took no proper and sufficient measures to investigate her character and to prevent the violation of the laws of the kingdom. She sailed from Liverpool without obstruction, cleared by the name of *Oreto*, unarmed, it is true, but accompanied by another vessel containing her armament, called the *Bahama*.

The *Oreto* next makes her appearance at Nassau, where she proceeded further to equip and arm as a man-of-war. The naval authorities at Nassau were unanimous in denouncing her illegal character, but the civil authorities, perverted by their *sympathies*, could with difficulty be persuaded to act against her. When they did act, she was acquitted by the local Admiralty Court, in the teeth of the facts and the law, either corruptly, or with inexplicable ignorance of their duty on the part of the Court and of the attorney representing the Government. No appeal was taken by the Government.

The *Oreto* then threw off all pretensions of innocence; she openly completed her equipment, armament, and crew, partly at one place and partly at another, under the eye of the colonial authorities; and proceeded to cruise and to make prizes as an avowed man-of-war by the name of *Florida*. Meanwhile, with the illegality of her operations in England, and also in the Bahama Islands, now notorious and admitted, she continued to come and go in British ports, and to obtain supplies there as her base of operations, without interference on the part of the British Government.

On these facts, the three neutral Arbitrators and Mr. Adams convicted the British Government of want of due diligence, and of disregard otherwise of the Rules of the Treaty, notwithstanding that the *Florida* had entered and remained some time in the Confederate port of Mobile.

Their several opinions were precise, definite, clear, and with positive conclusion, as to all the material points of the case, in favor of the United States.

Sir Alexander Cockburn's adverse opinion was a verbose special plea,—which, while admitting all the material facts charged, and conceding the palpable fraud practiced by Miller & Sons and Thomas,—the original guilt of the vessel,—the absurdity of the action of the Admiralty Court of Nassau,—the illegal equipments at Nassau and elsewhere in British ports, —and the continued use of British ports as a base of operations,—could not discover in these incidents any negligence or any violation of neutrality on the part of the British Government. Sir Alexander chose not to remember that the affair of the *Oreto* or *Florida* was, from the beginning to the end, according to the confession of Lord John Russell himself, a scandal and a reproach to the laws of Great Britain, and still more, we may add, a scandal and a reproach to certain of the British Ministers, of whose honor Sir Alexander assumes to be the special champion.

When Count Sclopis had concluded the reading of his opinion, Sir Alexander Cockburn renewed his motion for the hearing of Counsel; but was again overruled by the Tribunal, which assigned for its next Conference the consideration of the case of the *Alabama*.

SPECIAL ARGUMENTS ORDERED ON CERTAIN POINTS.

The Tribunal met again on the 25th; and the Baron d'Itajubá then made a precise and formal proposition, calling on the Counsel of Great Britain for a written or printed Statement or Argument in elucidation of three questions of law, namely:

" 1. The question of due diligence treated in a general manner.

" 2. The effect of commissions possessed by Confederate vessels of war which had entered into British ports.

" 3. The supplies of coal furnished to Confederate vessels in British ports."

And with liberty to the Counsel of the United States to reply either orally or in writing as the case may be.

This proposition was adopted by the Tribunal.

In so far as regards the first point, the call for Argument was obviously induced by a desire to put an end to the unseemly importunities of Sir Alexander Cockburn; for the Arbitrators had in effect again and again declared that in their judgment there was no occasion for elucidation or further discussion of the general question of due diligence; that the Tribunal did not desire any theoretical discussions of abstract questions; and that the practical question of due diligence had been already discussed to satiety in the several Cases and Arguments filed by the respective Governments. We shall perceive in the sequel how well-founded were the objections of the Tribunal in this respect; and how devoid of any useful object or purpose had been the ill-digested calls of Sir Alexander Cockburn.

To the other questions propounded by the Baron d'Itajubá, no objection could be made: they were fit subjects of the "elucidation" contemplated by the Treaty.

CASE OF THE "ALABAMA" DECIDED.

The Arbitrators then proceeded to read alphabetically their opinions in the case of the *Alabama*,—that is to say, Mr. Adams, Sir Alexander Cockburn, Count Sclopis, and Mr. Stæmpfli read argumentative statements at length, and the Baron d'Itajubá expressed his concurrence in the statement made by Sir Alexander Cockburn.

In this case the Arbitrators were unanimously of opinion,—the British Arbitrator equally with his colleagues,—that the British Government had been guilty of culpable want of the due diligence required, either by the law of nations, the Rules of the Treaty, or Act of Parliament.

In fact, this vessel had been built and fitted out in Great Britain in violation of her laws, with intent to carry on war against the United States; evidence of this fact had been submitted, sufficient, in the opinion of the Law Officers of the Crown, to justify her detention; notwithstanding which, by reason of absence of due vigilance, and not without suspicion of connivance on the part of public officers, and with extraordinary delay in issuing necessary orders, she was suffered to go unmolested out of the immediate jurisdiction of the British Government. Her armament, supplies, and crew were all procured from Great Britain. And, in like violation of law, she was received and treated as a legitimate man-of-war in the colonial ports of Great Britain.

Sir Alexander Cockburn was constrained to admit want of due diligence as to the case of the *Alabama*, in three distinct classes of facts, each one of which sufficed to establish the responsibility of the British Government.

If Sir Alexander had any good cause to accuse his colleagues, as he did, of precipitancy and want of knowledge or practice of law, because they came to provisional conclusions in the case of the *Florida* without waiting to hear Sir Roundell Palmer, surely the British Government had reason to attach the same censure to him in the case of the *Alabama*.

How could he presume to condemn Great Britain in this behalf, ignorantly, blindly, in the dark, and without assistance of the "reasoning and learning" of the eminent Counsel in attendance on the Tribunal?

But even Sir Alexander Cockburn could no longer resist the force of conviction, nor help admitting the truth of the allegation of the United States, their Agent and Counsel, imputing culpable negligence to his Government. The United States had, not without cause, brought the British Government to the bar of public opinion and of the Tribunal of Arbitration; himself now confessing it, their Agent and Counsel had not been engaged, as he had charged, in preferring "false accusations, unworthy of them and of their Government." And if the proved and admitted truth of these accusations implies impeachment of the *personal honor* of any British Minister or Ministers, that is not the fault of the American Government, its Agent or Counsel, but of the British Government, whose violation of neutrality is at length conceded even by Sir Alexander Cockburn.

In the ultimate judgment of *all* the Arbitrators, the condemnation of the *Alabama* and the *Florida* carried with it the condemnation of their respective tenders, namely, the *Tuscaloosa*, the *Clarence*, the *Tacony*, and the *Archer*.

CASE OF THE "SHENANDOAH" DECIDED.

There remained but three vessels as to whose responsibility we had reason to have hopes, namely, the *Georgia*, the *Retribution*, and the *Shenandoah*;

and with confident expectation only as to the *Shenandoah* after she left Melbourne. Without pausing here to consider particularly the *Retribution* and the *Georgia*, suffice it to say that eventually they were rejected; but the *Shenandoah*, after special explanations in writing submitted by the Counsel of the two Governments, was held responsible by vote of three of the Arbitrators, Count Sclopis, Mr. Stæmpfli, and Mr. Adams. As the *Shenandoah*, after increasing her armament at Melbourne, had made many captures at the very close of the war, when her cruise could not be of any possible advantage to the Confederates, her exoneration by the Tribunal would have been justly regarded by us as an act of great injustice to the United States.

THE SPECIAL ARGUMENTS.

It remains next to speak of the successive Arguments of Counsel before the Tribunal, as well those heretofore indicated as others called for in the sequel.

On the 25th of July, as we have seen, the Tribunal voted to require from the Counsel of Great Britain a written or printed Argument touching certain points.

On the 29th, Lord Tenterden announced that he had delivered the required Argument of the British Counsel to the Secretary of the Tribunal.

The copy thus delivered was in manuscript. As subsequently printed, it consists of 43 folio pages.

The replies of the American Counsel, each of them addressing the Tribunal separately, were presented on the 5th, 6th, and 8th of August, consisting altogether of 47 pages of the same folio impression.

It would not be convenient, and it does not come within my plan, to discuss the Arguments of Counsel on either side, except where some particular point of such Argument calls for notice. Hence, as in the case of the general Arguments of April and of June, so as to the special Arguments called for by the Tribunal, it will be sufficient to enumerate them, and to give to them their proper place in the history of the Arbitration.

The first Argument of Sir Roundell Palmer, however, calls for some observations.

Of his 43 pages, 31,—say three quarters,—are devoted *nominally* to the question of due diligence generally considered.

Now, in the previous regular Arguments, each Government had fully discussed this question, and had, as if by common consent, concluded in express terms that it neither required nor admitted any further discussion. That conclusion was correct. Accordingly, most of these 31 pages are occupied with matters remotely, if at all, connected with the question, What *constitutes* due diligence?—such as [copying, word for word, sundry marginal notes] rules and principles of international law; express or implied engagements of Great Britain; effect of prohibitory municipal laws; the three Rules of the Treaty; the maxims cited by the United States from Sir Robert Phillimore on the question, *Civitas ne deliquerit an cives;* for what purpose Great Britain refers to her municipal laws; doctrine of Tetens as to municipal laws in excess of antecedent international obligations; the arguments as to the prerogative powers belonging to the British Crown; the true doctrine as to the powers of the Crown under British law; the British Crown has power by common law to use the civil, military, and naval forces of the Realm to stop acts of war within British territory; the preventive powers of British law explained; examination of the preventive powers of the American Government under the Acts of Congress for the preservation of neutrality:—and so of diverse other questions discussed by Sir Roundell Palmer under the head of due diligence generally considered. Very *generally*, it is clear. Nay, 13 of the 31 pages devoted to the question of "due diligence generally considered" are occupied with examination of the laws and political history of the United States, in continuance and iteration of the groundless and irrelevant accusations of the American Government introduced into the British Case and Counter-Case.

Now Sir Roundell Palmer is, *omnium consensu*, at the head of the British Bar in learning, intelligence, and integrity; and we may be sure that arguments addressed by him to the Tribunal would be the best that such a lawyer, so high in mental and moral qualities, or that any living lawyer, be he who he may, could devise or conceive. The British Arbitrator had gone "clean daft" in the hope deferred of hearing him. He himself had been earnestly seeking to be heard by the Tribunal for more than a month; he had comtemplated being heard for many months. And the result of all this meditation, and of all this earnest desire to serve his country, was a series of arguments mostly immaterial to the issue, as the final judgment of the Tribunal plainly shows, and coming in after the main question had been actually settled in the cases of the *Alabama* and the *Florida*. That is to say,—and it is in this relation the point is introduced,—the claims of the United States rested on a basis which all the great forensic skill and ability of Sir Roundell Palmer could not move,—which commended itself to the confidence of the neutral Arbitrators,—and which even extorted the reluctant adhesion of the prejudiced British Arbitrator.

Subsequently, on requirement of the Arbitrators, we discussed, in successive printed Arguments, the special question of the legal effect of the entry of the *Florida* into Mobile; the question of the recruitment of men for the *Shenandoah* at Melbourne; and the question of interest as an element of the indemnity due to the United States.

QUESTION OF DAMAGES.

Meanwhile, the Tribunal had voted definitively on the question of the liability or non-liability of Great Britain for the acts of the cruisers named in the "Case" of the United States, in the terms which will appear in explaining their final judgment. They had also voted on several of the incidental questions, such as the abstract question of due diligence, entry into Confederate ports, commission, and supply of coal, raised by successive requirements of the Tribunal. They had thus arrived at the point of discussing matters, which only affected the form and the amount of the judgment to be rendered against Great Britain.

And here, on the 26th of August, the Tribunal voted to deliberate with closed doors, in spite of the objection of Sir Alexander Cockburn.

Thenceforth, and until the final Conference of the 14th of September, the Tribunal sat with closed doors, that is, without the assistance of the Agents and Counsel.

Down to this time, the Agent, Counsel, Solicitor, and Secretaries of the United States had been assiduously occupied in preparing, copying, translating, and printing Arguments and other documents for the use of the Tribunal. And even when the regular discussions were ended, we had still to attend to the laborious task of preparing schedules of the claims of the United States in response to argumentative estimates filed by the British Government.

FINAL JUDGMENT OF THE TRIBUNAL.

On the 9th of September the Arbitrators definitively adopted the Act of Decision, which had been considered at the preceding Conference, and ordered it to be printed. They also resolved that the Decision should be signed at the next Conference, to be held with open doors, and they then adjourned to the 14th.

ANNOUNCEMENT OF THE DECISION.

On Saturday, the 14th of September, the Tribunal assembled at the hour of adjournment,—half-past twelve o'clock. The Hall of Conference was crowded at this hour with the Arbitrators and the gentlemen attached to the Arbitration, the ladies of their respective families, the members of the Cantonal Government, representatives of the Press of Switzerland, the United States, and Great Britain, and gentlemen and ladies among the most estimable of the private citizens of Geneva. The day was beautiful; the scene imposing and impressive. But the British Arbitrator, Sir Alexander Cockburn, remained unaccountably absent, while curiosity grew into impatience, and impatience into apprehension, until long after the prescribed hour of meeting, when the British Arbitrator finally made his appearance.

The official action of the Conference commenced with the accustomed formalities.

The President then presented the Act of Decision of the Tribunal, and directed the Secretary to read it in English, which was done: after which duplicate originals of the Act were signed by Mr. Adams, Count Frederic Sclopis, Mr. Stæmpfli, and Viscount of Itajubá; and a copy of the Decision, thus signed, was delivered to each of the Agents of the two Governments respectively.

Another original was subscribed in like manner, to be placed, together with the archives of the Tribunal, among the archives of the Council of State of the Canton of Geneva.

Sir Alexander Cockburn, as one of the Arbitrators, declining to assent to the Decision, presented a statement of his "Reasons," which, without reading, the Tribunal ordered to be received and recorded.

Thereupon, in an appropriate address, Count Sclopis declared the labors of the Arbitrators to be finished, and the Tribunal dissolved.

The discourse of Count Sclopis was immediately followed by *salvos* of artillery, discharged from the neighboring site of La Treille by order of the Cantonal Government, with display of the flags of Geneva and of Switzerland between those of the United States and of Great Britain.

It is impossible that any one of the persons present on that occasion should ever lose the impression of the moral grandeur of the scene, where the actual rendition of arbitral judgment on the claims of the United States against Great Britain bore witness to the generous magnanimity of two of the greatest nations of the world in resorting to peaceful reason as the arbiter of grave national differences, in the place of indulging in baneful resentments or the vulgar ambition of war. This emotion was visible on almost every countenance, and was manifested by the exchange of amicable salutations appropriate to the separation of so many persons, who, month after month, had been seated side by side as members of the Tribunal, or as Agents and Counsel of the two Governments; for even the adverse Agents and Counsel had contended with courteous weapons, and had not, on either side, departed, intentionally or consciously, from the respect due to themselves, to one another, and to their respective Governments.

CONDUCT OF THE BRITISH ARBITRATOR.

To the universal expression of mutual courtesy and reciprocal good-will there was but one exception, and that exception too conspicuous to pass without notice.

The instant that Count Sclopis closed, and before the sound of his last words had died on the ear, Sir Alexander Cockburn snatched up his hat, and, without participating in the exchange of leave-takings around him, without a word or sign of courteous recognition for any of his colleagues, rushed to the door and disappeared, in the manner of a criminal escaping from the dock, rather than of a judge separating, and that forever, from his colleagues of the Bench. It was one of those acts of discourtesy which shock so much when they occur that we feel relieved by the disappearance of the perpetrator.

SIR ALEXANDER COCKBURN'S REASONS FOR DISSENT.

The British Arbitrator, who, so frequently in the course of the Conferences, acted as a party agent rather than a judge, had been occupying himself in the preparation of a long Argument on the side of Great Britain, in which he throws off the mask, and *professedly* speaks as the representative of the British Government. He withheld this Argument from the knowledge of the Tribunal at the proper time for its presentation as the "Reasons" of an *Arbitrator*. At the last moment,—without its being read to the

Tribunal, or printed for the information of Agents and Counsel, as a resolution of the Tribunal, adopted on his own motion, required,—he presents this Argument as his "Reasons . . . for dissenting from the Decision of the Tribunal of Arbitration." The title of the document is a false pretense, as we shall conclusively show in due time: the act was a dishonorable imposition on the Tribunal, and on *both* Governments, Great Britain as much as the United States.

In point of fact, the document filed by Sir Alexander was in large part of such a character that, if it had been offered for filing at any proper time, and with opportunity to persons concerned to become acquainted with its contents, it must [as declared by the Secretary of State of the United States in his dispatch to the American Agent of October 22, 1872] have been the plain duty of the American Agent to object to its reception, and of the Tribunal to refuse it, as calculated and designed to weaken the just authority of the Arbitrators, as insulting to the United States in the tenor of much of its contents, and as injurious to Great Britain by its tendency to raise up obstacles to the acceptance of the Award, and to produce alienation between the two Governments.

The document consisted, in part, of the opinions of Sir Alexander Cockburn on the several vessels, copies of which he ought to have delivered in print to the Agent and Counsel of the United States, in conformity with his own resolution, but which he failed to do, thus depriving the American Government of advantages in this relation to which it was entitled, and which the British Government in fact enjoyed by reason of the more loyal conduct of the other Arbitrators.

He discusses these vessels with great prolixity, so as to fill 180 pages folio letter-press, while the correspondent opinions of all the other Arbitrators united occupy only 66 pages, the difference being occasioned partly by the number of letters and other papers interjected into his opinions, and partly by the diffuseness and looseness of his style and habit of thought, as compared with theirs.

The residue of Sir Alexander's document, consisting of 116 pages, is devoted partly to the discussion of the special questions, in all which he is inordinately prolix, and partly to a general outpouring of all the bile which had been accumulating on his stomach during the progress of the Arbitration.

SIR ALEXANDER COCKBURN'S "REASONS."

Let me dispose once for all of these "Reasons" and their author, in order to arrive at subjects of more importance and interest. The matter of the document, and the consideration it has received in England, require that it should be examined and judged from an American stand-point.

Apart from the unjudicial violence and extravagance of these "Reasons," it is remarkable how inconsistent, how self-contradicting, how destitute of logical continuity of thought, how false as reasoning, as well as irrelevant, is most of the matter.

The Reasons are on their face, and as the London Press could not fail to perceive and admit, " an elaborate reply to the American Case" [that is to say, an advocate's plea], "rather than a judicial verdict." [*Telegraph,* September 25.]

It is, in truth, a mere *nisi prius* argument, not up to the level of an argument in *banc;* inappropriate to the character of a judge; and which might have been quite in place at Geneva as an "Argument" in the cause, provided any British Counsel could have been found to write so acrimoniously and reason so badly as Sir Alexander.

To establish these positions, it would suffice to cite some of the criticisms of the London Press.

The *Telegraph* [September 26] argumentatively demonstrates the palpable fallacy of the reasoning by which Sir Alexander endeavors to excuse the admitted violation of law and the want of due diligence of the British Government in the case of the *Florida,* especially at Nassau.

The *News* [September 26] condemns and regrets the declaration made by Sir Alexander in his "Reasons" twice, where he speaks of himself "sitting on the Tribunal as in some sense the representative of Great Britain," and contrasts this with the sounder view of his duty expressed in Parliament by Lord Cairns.

Compare, now, this observation of the *News* with certain pertinent remarks of the *Telegraph* [September 25]. Speaking of Mr. Adams, it says: "He put aside the temper of the advocate when he took his seat on the Bench, and he performed the difficult duty with the impartiality of a jurist and *the delicate honor of a gentleman*." And this well-merited commendation of Mr. Adams is prefatory to the exhibition of Sir Alexander Cockburn retaining still " the temper of an advocate when *he* took his seat on the Bench," and *not* performing his duties "with the impartiality of a jurist and the delicate honor of a gentleman," but to the contrary, as shown by his deportment at Geneva, and authenticated under his own hand in these " Reasons."

There is no escape from the dilemma: it was honorable to Mr. Adams to act as a "judge" at Geneva; and, of course, to act as a mere " advocate " was dishonorable to Sir Alexander Cockburn.

And thus we may comprehend at a glance, what seems so remarkable to the *Telegraph* [September 26], that when we pass from the printed opinions of the three neutral Arbitrators, whose " fairness " nobody disputes, and from those of the impartial "jurist" and honorable " gentleman," Mr. Charles Francis Adams, to the "Reasons" of Sir Alexander Cockburn, " We seem to go into another climate of opinion. . . . We find different premises, a different bias, a different logic, and we might almost say different facts." So it is, indeed; and the explanation is obvious. The "climate" of Count Sclopis, Baron d'Itajubá, Mr. Stæmpfli, and Mr. Adams, was that of fairness, judicial dignity, impartiality; gentlemanly honor, such as belonged to their place as Arbitrators: the "climate" of Sir Alexander Cockburn was that of a self-appointed "advocate," making no pretensions to "fairness" or "impartiality," but, with the "premises," "bias," "logic," and "facts" of such an advocate, drawing up a passionate, rhetorical plea, as the officious "representative of Great Britain."

As such "representative of Great Britain," if he be not promptly disavowed by the British Government, it will be found that his "Reasons" lay down many positions which may somewhat embarrass present or subsequent Ministers.

The *News* notices numerous contradictory opinions or conclusions which appear in the "Reasons." In one place Sir Alexander complains that *any* Rules are laid down by the Treaty, and in another place expresses the conviction that it is well to settle such questions by Treaty Rules. "He complains . . . that the Arbitrators have not been left free to apply the hitherto received principles of international law, and that they have; that rules have been laid down, and that they have not; that definitions have been framed, and that they have not been framed." Here is most exquisite confusion of ideas. It is the very same extraordinary and characteristic method of thinking and writing which Mr. Finlason had exhibited at length, and which Mr. Gathorne Hardy pointed out in the case of the Queen against Norton: the "inflammatory statements,"—the "extra-judicial denunciation," the "extra-judicial declamation," the going "from one side to another," and the saying "it is" and "it is not" upon every point of law. The perfect similitude of these repulsive features of the "Charge" and the "Reasons" can not be accidental: it must have its cause in idiosyncrasies of mental constitution.

This vacillation or contradictoriness of opinion, which strikes the *News* so much, pervades the "Reasons."

Thus Sir Alexander admits want of due diligence in the matter of the *Alabama*, and yet stoutly denies that the United States had any good cause of complaint against Great Britain. He insists that Ministers were to officiate within the limits of municipal law, and yet admits that such is not the law of nations, the force of which he also recognizes. He denies that the Ministers can lawfully exercise any prerogative power in such matters, and yet justifies and approves the exercise of it [although too late] in the case of the *Shenandoah*.

The *News* also calls attention to Sir Alexander's "disaffection to the conditions under which he discharges his task, a task voluntarily accepted with full knowledge of those conditions." "He criticises adversely the Treaty of Washington: . . . these criticisms seem to us to be *extra vires*. A derived authority ought surely to respect its source. . . . Other considerations than those laid down for him have certainly been present to the mind of Sir Alexander Cockburn," etc.

There is manifest justness in this criticism. What business had Sir Alexander to indulge in continual crimination of the Treaty of Washington, while acting as Arbitrator under it, and possessing no power or jurisdiction except such as the Treaty confers? To do so was indecent in itself, and could have no effect other than to embarrass the British Government. With his habitual inconsistency of thought, to be sure, he advises submission to the judgment of the Arbitrators, while exhausting himself in efforts to shake its moral strength and that of the Treaty. The *Times* [September 28] plainly sees that the "Reasons" of Sir Alexander "will be duly turned to account by Opposition critics." And perhaps that was one of the objects Sir Alexander had in view, in thus usurping the function to judge the Treaty under the cover of acting as Arbitrator to judge the specific questions submitted by the Treaty.

The *Times* admits that the "severity of the criticism passed by the Chief Justice *on the United States* and their Agents, and *even on his colleagues*, may, from a diplomatic point of view, be some ground for regret;" . . . that "perhaps he was too ready to consider himself the representative of England;" that "perhaps he takes more than a judicial pleasure" in one argumentative suggestion; and that "he dwells, perhaps, with something too much of the delight of an advocate" on some other point; and in each one of these admissions, qualified as they are, we perceive recognition of the fact that, in his "Reasons," Sir Alexander does not speak as an international Arbitrator, or manifest the qualities which ought to characterize a Chief Justice.

The *News* indicates other singular traits of "irrelevance" and confusion of mind in the "Reasons."

Examination of the substance of the "Reasons" leads to still more unfavorable conclusions.

While the Chief Justice exhausts himself in fault-finding with the Counsel of the United States, it is observable that he seldom, if ever, grapples with their arguments, but shoots off instead into epithets of mere vituperation. Indeed, if it were worth while, it would be easy to show that he did not really read that which he so intemperately criticises. And when he undertakes to deal with the text, it is only in the disingenuous manner of picking out here and there a detached paragraph or phrase for comment, regardless of the context or the general line of argument.

Nevertheless, when he has occasion to differ in opinion with the Counsel of the United States, such is the perverted state of passion and prejudice in which he thinks and writes, that he imputes to us intention to *practice* on the "supposed credulity and ignorance" of the Tribunal.

We were not amenable in anywise to the British Arbitrator; but, if we had been barristers in his own Court of whom such things were said by him, it would have been an example of judicial indecency to parallel which it would be necessary to go back to the days of infamous judges like Jeffreys or Scroggs.

Let Sir Alexander be judged by his own rule. *Cramming*, as he did at Geneva, in the preparation of his "Reasons," he examined superficially and wrote precipitately: in consequence of which he copied from the Arguments for the British Government palpable errors, which were exposed and corrected in the Arguments for the United States. Thus it is that he falls into the mistake of asserting a false construction of an Act of Congress, by having a mutilated text before him, quoting a *part* of a sentence, which may or may not justify his construction, and suppressing the context and the sequent words of the same sentence, which clearly contradict his construction. Acting on his own theory of blind prejudice, we should be compelled to assume that on this occasion he perpetrates a deed of deliberate bad faith, with intention to *practice* on the " supposed credulity and ignorance" of the people of Great Britain.

Why did the British Arbitrator put together such a mass of angry, irrelevant, confused, and contradictory declamation against the American Government, and denunciation of its Agent and Counsel? To vindicate the *honor* of British statesmen, Sir Alexander declares, in a speech at a banquet in London [November 4th], against unjust charges coming from the American Government. But that should have been done by speech or otherwise, as *Sir Alexander Cockburn* professedly, and in England, and not under the false pretense of an Arbitrator at Geneva. And violent denunciation of our Case or Arguments constitutes no answer to our charges. And in such vituperation of the American Agent and Counsel, Sir Alexander not only throws off all pretense of judicial character, and assumes the tone of a mere advocate, but he acts the part of an advocate in temper and manner such as the proper Counsel of the British Government could not have descended to. Indeed, the

"Reasons" proceed from beginning to end on the hypothesis that the British Agent and Counsel had neglected their duty; that neither the Case, Counter-Case, nor Argument of the British Government, by whomsoever prepared, nor the several supplementary Arguments filed by Sir Roundell Palmer in his own name, contained a proper exhibition of the defenses of the British Government; and more especially that Agent and Counsel alike had all been false to their country's *honor* in not vindicating it against the charges of the Americans. In view of this dereliction of duty, Sir Alexander volunteers to supply, *more suo*, the place of Counsel, and to respond to the American Agent and Counsel.

Against what charges? The existence of an unfriendly state of mind toward the American Government in Parliament, or in some of the British Colonies at the period in question? Sir Alexander admits the fact in stronger terms than we had charged it.—Failure to exercise due diligence in arresting the equipment of Confederate cruisers to depredate on our commerce? Sir Alexander admits and proves it, under three heads, as to the *Alabama*, and only escapes the same admission as to the *Florida* by technicalities as unsatisfactory to impartial minds in England as in America.—As the London *Telegraph* says, in another relation, Sir Alexander, whilst indignantly protesting against our accusation of British officers, admits their failure to do their duty, which is the foundation of the accusation. But for that marvelous confusion of ideas which distinguishes Sir Alexander, even he must have seen that, in confessing and *proving* the guilt of his Government, he estops himself from denying the justice of the accusation preferred by the United States.

But the point of honor was considered when the Treaty was signed. How strangely Sir Alexander forgets the attitude in which this objection stands in Lord Russell's correspondence with Mr. Adams. If there was any question of honor in the controversy, that it was which forbade a treaty of arbitration, as Lord Russell constantly maintained. But three successive Foreign Ministries, represented by Lord Stanley, Lord Clarendon, and Lord Granville, had rightly decided that the question at issue did not involve the honor of the British Government. Sir Alexander wastes his words over a dead issue, utterly buried out of sight by the stipulations of the Treaty of Washington.

Mr. John Lemoinne expresses the judgment of Europe, and anticipates that of history, in condemning Sir Alexander's "vehemence of polemic and bitterness of discussion, so extraordinary in an official document."

Strangely enough, the *Saturday Review*, which pretends to see "scurrility" in the American Case and Argument, where it does not exist, is blind to it in the "Reasons," where it is a flagrant fact.

Meanwhile, there is nothing accusatory of Great Britain in the American Case,—there is nothing of earnest inculpation of the British Government in the American Argument,—which is not greatly exceeded by extra-judicial accusation and inculpation of the United States in the "Reasons" of Sir Alexander.

And it is amusing to read the imputations of "confusion," "vague and declamatory," "ignorance of law and history," which he applies to the American Counsel, in view of what his own countrymen say of his own methods of argumentation. Indeed, it would seem that the hard words of Mr. Finlason and others concerning him had made such effectual lodgment in his brain that, whenever he writes, they rush forth hap-hazard to be applied by him without reason or discrimination to any occasional object of argument or controversy.

If, like Mr. Charles Francis Adams, Sir Alexander had simply prepared brief and temperate opinions on all the questions, whether favorable or not to the United States, both Governments would have been left in an amicable mood. As it is, in professedly throwing off the character of a judge,—which alone belonged to him of right,—of certain specific charges of the United States against Great Britain, submitted to him by the Treaty of Washington,—and in undertaking to become the mere accuser of the United States,—he does but insult the American Government, while subjecting his own Government to much present inconvenience and great future embarrassment.

There is one particular feature of the "Reasons" too remarkable to be overlooked.

In reading these "Reasons" carefully, one can not fail to be struck by the frequent manifestation of the disposition of Sir Alexander Cockburn to stop and turn aside in order to criticise Mr. Stæmpfli.

Mr. Stæmpfli, in conformity with the vote of the Tribunal, printed his *provisional* opinions, and delivered them to the other Arbitrators, from time to time, and to the respective Agents and Counsel.

Sir Alexander Cockburn disingenuously suppressed his provisional opinions until the last moment, and then filed a *single* copy only of the mass of matter, general and special, entitled "Reasons," which appears in print for the first time in the London *Gazette*.

Now, in the provisional opinions of Mr. Stæmpfli, it is quite possible there may have been some error of statement. Sir Alexander takes pains to affirm it. But, if there be any such, it is quite immaterial, and does not affect any important conclusion either of fact or of law.

Sir Alexander also committed errors of this class in the provisional opinions *which he read*. Some of them were noted at the time, and are still remembered. These errors may have been corrected in the print which we now have. Indeed, the *manuscript* shows numerous corrections. Nevertheless, but for the suppression of *his* provisional opinions, his colleagues might have interlarded their provisional or revised opinions with similar captious criticisms of him. It is presumable that they did not think it becoming or fair to do this; and it was to the last degree unfair in Sir Alexander to do it, in a document foisted into the record, as it was, at the instant of adjournment, and *immediately carried off* without being actually filed with the Secretary or otherwise placed in the archives of the Tribunal.

Now, in the early pages of his " Reasons," he imputes to Mr. Stæmpfli the having said " that there is no such thing as international law, and that consequently we [the Arbitrators] are to proceed independently of any such law," and " according to some intuitive perception of right and wrong or speculative notions, etc."

The imputation is calumnious. No such statement appears in any of the printed opinions of Mr. Stæmpfli; no such declaration was ever made by him orally at any of the Conferences. The declaration of Sir Alexander in this respect is but a sample of the rashness and inaccuracy of representation· which pervade the " Reasons."

What Mr. Stæmpfli says on the general subject of "international law," in so far as regards the matters before the Tribunal, is as follows:

" Principes généraux de droit.

" Dans ses considérants juridiques, le Tribunal doit se guider par les principes suivants:—

" 1. En premier lieu, par les trois Règles posées dans l'Article VI. du Traité, lequel porte que,—et cetera.

. . . . .

" D'après le Traité ces trois Règles prévalent sur les principes que l'on pourrait déduire du droit des gens historique et de la science.

" 2. Le droit des gens historique, ou bien la pratique du droit des gens, ainsi que la science et les autorités scientifiques, peuvent être considérés comme droit subsidiaire, en tant que les principes à appliquer sont généralement reconnus et ne sont point sujets à controverse, ni en désaccord avec les trois Règles cidessus. Si l'une ou l'autre de ces conditions vient à manquer, c'est au Tribunal d'y suppléer en interprétant et appliquant les trois Règles de son mieux et en toute conscience."

At the time when Sir Alexander sent to press his misrepresentation of the opinions of Mr. Stæmpfli, he had in his hands the authentic statement thereof as printed at Geneva. There is no excuse, therefore, for this malicious and dishonorable endeavor of the British Arbitrator to prejudice the character of the Swiss Arbitrator in Great Britain.

Nevertheless, Mr. Stæmpfli, according to Sir Alexander, having cut adrift from all positive law, adopts instead "speculative notions," or "some *intuitive* perception of right and wrong;" and such ideas Sir Alexander repudiates: or, as the London *Telegraph* has it, "the Chief Justice, armed with sarcasm as well as logic, runs full tilt against *that* doctrine:" to wit, the doctrine, still in the words of the *Telegraph*, "that the duties which nations owe to each other must be determined by the light of intuitive principles of justice." The *Telegraph* goes on, with truth and reason, to say that, after all, Mr. Stæmpfli is right, if he insists that "the rules of fair dealing, which we term international law, are not law *in the same sense* as the positive edicts of the common law; for the essence of such edicts is that they come from a lawgiver in the form of a parliament or a sovereign: the rules of international justice are simply the code which experience and the judgment of able men have shown to be fair or expedient, but every civilized country feels them to be not less binding on that account." Without pausing to consider whether these observations are perfectly accurate or not as a definition of the law of nations, we may assume that they are substantially so, and suffice at any rate to show clearly the uncandid spirit of Sir Alexander's criticism of the imputed language of Mr. Stæmpfli,—a criticism which calls to mind a similar unjust and vicious reproach cast by Junius on Lord Mansfield.

The actual statement of Mr. Stæmpfli, as we have seen, was unexceptionably accurate and precise, in so far as regarded the matters before the Tribunal.

Meanwhile, Mr. Stæmpfli may have said orally, what he says here in print, that in many supposable cases of deficient explicitness either of the conventional rules or of the historic law of nations, " c'est au Tribunal d'y suppléer en interprétant et appliquant les trois règles de son mieux et *en toute conscience.*"

That is what the Viscount of Itajubá says in one of his opinions, namely, that a certain doctrine, asserted by the British Government, " froisse la conscience." It is what Count Sclopis intends, when he says, " Les nations ont entre elles un droit commun, ou, si on aime mieux, un lien commun, *formé par l'équité* et sanctionné par le respect des intérêts réciproques;" and that such is the spirit of the Treaty of Washington, " qui ne fait que donner la préférence aux règles de l'équité générale sur les dispositions d'une législation particulière quelle qu'elle puisse être." That is " the universal immutable justice," which in all systems of law, international or national, distinguishes right from wrong, and to which the United States appealed in addressing the Tribunal of Arbitration. And it is the negation of all these great principles of "justice," "equity," or "conscience," which pervades the "Reasons" of Sir Alexander Cockburn: in reflecting on which, the mind irresistibly reverts to that same line of reasoning which astonished the world in his parliamentary advocacy of David Pacifico.

And now, who is injured by Sir Alexander's acrimonious arraignment of the United States in the last hour of the Arbitration? It does not successfully maintain the *honor* of the British Ministers; for it recognizes their failure to exercise due diligence, whether tried by the Treaty Rules, by the law of nations, or by the Act of Parliament. Does it influence the action of the Tribunal? No: that was consummated already. Does it injure the American Government, its Agent and Counsel? No: so far as regards us, it does but prove that the American Agent and Counsel have done their duty regardless of the vindictive ill-will of the British Arbitrator, and that the United States have been successful to such a degree as to throw the Chief Justice of England into ecstasies of spiteful rage, in which he strikes out wildly against friend and foe alike, but chiefly against his own Government, in his desultory criticism as well of the Treaty of Washington as of the judgment of the Tribunal of Arbitration.

For the British Government, we know, has no disposition to repudiate the Treaty, and it accepts the Award in good faith, and desires that it should be accepted by the people of Great Britain. It can not be

K

agreeable to the British Government to have all the old debate reopened by the Chief Justice,—to have the Treaty, its Rules, the Arbitration, and the Award, made by him the subject of profuse denunciation,—to have an arsenal of weapons, good, bad, or indifferent, collected by him for the use of the Opposition in Parliament.

Nor can it be agreeable to see the Arbitrator they had appointed demean himself so fantastically, and, as the English Press is constrained to admit, in a manner so painfully in contrast with the dignity and judicial impartiality of the American Arbitrator.

The Chancellor of the Exchequer [Mr. Lowe] gave utterance to these sentiments of grief and regret in a speech at Glasgow on the 26th of September, as follows:

"I conceive our duty to be to obey the Award, and to pay whatever is assessed against us without cavil or comment of any kind. [Cheers.] I am happy to say that such is the opinion of my learned friend, the Lord Chief Justice. But I must say, with the greatest submission to my learned friend, that I wish his practice had accorded a little more accurately with his theory. He has advised us to submit, as I advise you to submit, to the Award, and not only to pay the money, but to forego for once the national habit of grumbling—[laughter]—and to consider that we are bound in honor to do what we are told, and that, having once put the thing out of our power in the honorable and the high-minded way in which the nation has done, the only way in which we should treat it is simply to obey the Award, and to abstain from any comment whatever as to what the Arbitrators have done. [Cheers.] But, if my learned friend the Lord Chief Justice thought so, I can only very much regret that he did not take the course of simply signing the Award with the other Arbitrators, it being perfectly well known that he differed from them in certain respects, which would appear by the transactions of the Award. I think it is a pity when the thing is decided, when we are bound to act upon it, and when we are not really justified, in any feeling of honor or of good faith, in making any reclamation or quarrel at all with what has been done, that he should have thought it his duty to stir up and to renew all the strong arguments and contests upon which these Arbitrators have decided. [Cheers.] I think if it was his opinion that we ought to acquiesce quietly and without murmur in the Award, he had better not have published his argument, and, if he thought it right to publish his argument, he had better have retrenched his advice itself as to the arbitration."

Mr. Lowe can not help seeing that the "Reasons" are not an *opinion*, but an "argument," and an "argument" adverse to the conclusions of the writer.

Thus, it would appear, such is the eccentric mental constitution of the Chief Justice, that while he is incapable of going through any process of reasoning without inconsistencies and self-contradictions at every step, so he can not perform an act, or recommend its performance, without at the same time setting forth ample reasons to forbid its performance.

In the recent debate in Parliament, to be sure, on the Queen's speech, some of the members of both Houses, especially of those in Opposition, speak in terms of laudation of the "Reasons" of the Chief Justice. Lord Cairns, on this occasion, seems to have forgotten what he had said, on a previous occasion, of the judicial impartiality to be expected of an arbitrator. And Mr. Vernon Harcourt, in defending the Chief Justice against what the Chancellor of the Exchequer had said of him at Glasgow, unconsciously falls into the error of characterizing him as "the representative of the Crown, sent forth to discharge his duty to his Sovereign and maintain the honor of his country:" which affords to Mr. Lowe opportunity of responding triumphantly as follows:

"I have not spoken of the Lord Chief Justice in the language in which the honorable and learned gentleman has spoken of him, and which filled me with unbounded astonishment. The Lord Chief Justice was sent to Geneva as an Arbitrator to act impartially, and not to allow himself to be biased by the fact of his being an Englishman, but to give his judgment on what he thought to be the merits of the case. That is my belief with regard to the Lord Chief Justice, with regard to whom I am arraigned by the honorable and learned gentleman as having treated him disrespectfully. But how does the honorable and learned gentleman himself speak of the Lord Chief Justice? He says that learned Judge was a plenipotentiary,—that is to say, that he went to Geneva to do the work of England, and not to decide between two parties impartially, but to be biased in his course, and to go all lengths for England. The conduct of the Lord Chief Justice negatives such a statement, because in some respects the learned lord went against us. Then the honorable and learned gentleman said that the Lord Chief Justice was sent to Geneva to defend the honor of this country; but the fact is that *he was sent to arbitrate, and Sir Roundell Palmer and others were sent to defend the honor of the country. It would be a libel on the Lord Chief Justice to insinuate that he would undertake the office of going to Geneva nominally in the character of Arbitrator, but really to act as an advocate and plenipotentiary for this country.*"

It is difficult to judge how much of what Mr. Lowe said on this occasion was intended as sincere defense of the Chief Justice, and how much was mere sarcasm. But this uncertainty is due to the ambiguous and equivocal conduct of the Chief Justice himself, and to his own declaration that, while engaged in writing an extra-judicial pamphlet, under the false pretense of its being the act of an Arbitrator, he was really speaking as the Representative of Great Britain. That was the mistake of the Chief Justice. It was competent for him, after running away from the Tribunal as he did, to publish in England the contents of the first part of the "Reasons" as a personal act. It was dishonorable in him to smuggle it into the archives of the Tribunal, and to publish it in the London *Gazette* as the official act of an Arbitrator.

In view of all these incidents, and of the extraordinary contrast between the conduct of Mr. Adams and Sir Alexander Cockburn, as admitted by Englishmen themselves, it is easy to comprehend that, while the former has been honored with the express official commendation of *both* Governments, the latter, by wantonly insulting his fellow-Arbitrators and the United States, has, while receiving partisan praise in Parliament, rendered it difficult, if not impossible, for him to receive the hearty approval even of his own Government.

OPINIONS OF THE OTHER ARBITRATORS.

The other Arbitrators also placed on record their separate opinions as finally corrected, all which deserve notice. Each of these opinions consists of an affirmative exposition of the views of the Arbitrator who speaks. Count Sclopis, Mr. Stæmpfli, the Vicomte d'Itajubá, and Mr. Adams, each of them states his conclusions founded on the documents and arguments before the Tribunal. Neither of them seems to have imagined that the cause of truth or of justice would have been promoted by going outside of the documents and arguments submitted, in order to criticise or cavil at the opinions of the British Arbitrator.

We begin with Mr. Adams. His opinions are of some length; and, although containing correct statements of local law where such statements were material, yet deserve to be regarded in the better light of diplomacy and of international jurisprudence. He does not descend from the Bench into the arena of the Bar. If he had seen fit to do this, he might have discovered quite as much inducement to acrimony and acerbity of discussion in the wanton accusations of the entire political life of the United States, which the British Case, Counter-Case, and Argument contain, as Sir Alexander did in any thing which the Cases and Argument of the United States contained. But he yielded to no such temptation. "He put aside the temper of the advocate," as the *Telegraph* truly says, to speak "with the impartiality of a jurist and the delicate honor of a gentleman." Accordingly, his opinions are without blemish either in temper or in language. He finds want of due diligence in the matter of the *Alabama:* and so did the British Arbitrator. He finds extraordinary disregard of law in the matter of the *Florida:* and so did the British Arbitrator. He finds a series of acts of scandalous wrong perpetrated by officers of the British Government in both these cases: and so did the British Arbitrator. He can not, as the British Arbitrator does, find justification for the acts of negligence of British Colonial authorities in the matter of the *Shenandoah* or that of the *Retribution*. And, as might have been anticipated, his conception of the duties of a State suppose a higher standard of national morality than that recognized by the British Arbitrator.

Mr. Stæmpfli's opinions are also of considerable length, but differ from those of Mr. Adams, especially in the form, which is that customary among the jurists of the Continent. He also, while confining himself to the most rigorous deductions of international law, in discussing the acts of the inculpated Confederate cruisers, yet writes like a statesman, habituated to breathe the air of that "climate" of "the impartiality of a jurist and the delicate honor of a gentleman" which was *not* the "climate" of the British Arbitrator.

The opinions of the Vicomte d'Itajubá are very brief, but in the same form of analysis as the opinions of Mr. Stæmpfli. It is to be noted, however, that, beyond stating his reasoning and conclusion as to each of the inculpated cruisers, he speaks of only one of the special questions argued, namely, that of the effect to be given in British ports to the Confederate cruisers exhibiting commissions. As to this point he concludes as follows:

"La commission dont un tel navire est pourvu, ne suffit pas pour le couvrir vis-à-vis du neutre dont-il a violé la neutralité. Et comment le belligérant se plaindrait-il de l'application de ce principe? En saisissant ou détenant le navire, le neutre ne fait qu'empêcher le belligérant de tirer profit de *la fraude commise* sur son territoire par ce même belligérant; tandis que, en ne procédant point contre le navire coupable, le neutre s'expose justement à ce que l'autre belligérant *suspecte sa bonne foi.*"

In these observations, we see that the Vicomte d'Itajubá appeals to the same "intuitive perceptions of right" which are so unpalatable to the British Arbitrator.

The Vicomte d'Itajubá does not give us any opinion on the subject of " due diligence generally considered:" which tends to prove that his call for argument on that point was not induced by any need on his part for elucidation of Counsel.

The opinions of Count Sclopis,—not only those in which he judges the particular cases, but especially those in which he discusses the questions of public law, as to which mere *opinion* was drawn from the Arbitrators, virtually at the instance of Great Britain,— are instructive and interesting disquisitions, of permanent value as the views of an erudite legist and a practiced statesman. The paper on due diligence is remarkable for its profound and comprehensive view of that subject in its higher relation to the acts of sovereign States. In this paper, he thoroughly exposes the fallacy of the argument of Sir Roundell Palmer, which would lower the generality and the greatness of the Treaty Rules to the level of the municipal law of Great Britain.

And now, having reviewed the stipulations of the Treaty in this respect, the debates attending it both before and after its conclusion, the proceedings of the Tribunal of Arbitration, and the separate opinions of the Arbitrators, we come to the consideration of what they actually decided, the immediate effect of the Decision, and the general relation thereof to Great Britain, to the United States, and to the other Governments of Europe and America.

REVIEW OF THE DECISION OF THE TRIBUNAL ON NATIONAL LOSSES.

To begin, let us see what was the true thought of the Tribunal regarding the class of claims, as to which the British Government displayed so much superfluous emotion subsequently to the publication of the American Case, and which the Tribunal passed upon, in effect, without previous decision whether they were or were not embraced in the Treaty.

I have already called attention to the fact that no consideration of *direct* or *indirect, immediate* or *consequential,* appears in that opinion of the Tribunal. The Arbitrators express a *conclusion,* not the reasons of the conclusion. We might, it is true, easily infer those reasons from the language in which the conclusion is expressed. That language excludes all such trivial questions as whether "direct" or "indirect," and invokes us to seek for the unexpressed reasons in some higher order of ideas. Meanwhile we have, at length, in the final "Decision," means of ascertaining the whole thought of the Tribunal.

The Arbitrators had to pass on a claim of indemnity for the costs of pursuit of Confederate cruisers by the Government:—a claim admitted to be within the jurisdiction of the Tribunal, and which the Tribunal rejects on the ground that such costs "are not, in the judgment of the Tribunal, properly distinguishable from the general expenses of the war carried on by the United States."

Here, the major premise is assumed as already determined or admitted, namely, that "the general expenses of the war" are not to be made the subject of award. Why not? Because such expenses are in the nature of *indirect* losses? No such notion is intimated. Because the claim, as being for *indirect* losses, is not within the purview of the Treaty? That is not said or implied. Because such a claim is beyond the jurisdiction of the Tribunal? No: for the Tribunal takes jurisdiction and judges in fact. The question then remains,—why is a claim for losses pertaining to the general expenses of the war to be rejected?

There can be no mistake as to the true answer. It is to be found in the preliminary opinion expressed by the Arbitrators.

The Tribunal, in that opinion, says that the controverted [the so-called indirect] claims "do not constitute, upon the principles of international law applicable to such cases, good foundation for an award of compensation or computation of damages between nations." Why does not the injury done to a nation by the destruction of its commerce, and by the augmentation of the duration and expenses of war, constitute "a good foundation for an award of compensation or computation of damages between nations?" The answer is that such subjects of reclamation are "not properly distinguishable from the general expenses of war."

Let us analyze these two separate but related opinions, and thus make clear the intention of the Tribunal. It is this:

The injuries done to a Belligerent by the failure of a Neutral to exercise due diligence for the prevention of belligerent equipments in its ports, or the issue of hostile expeditions therefrom, in so far as they are injuries done to the Belligerent in its political capacity as a nation, and resolving themselves into an element of the national charges of war sustained by the Belligerent in its political capacity as a nation, do not, "upon the *principles of international law* applicable to such cases" [excluding, that is, the three Rules], constitute "good foundation for an award of compensation or computation of damages between nations."

Such, in my opinion, is the thought of the Arbitrators, partially expressed in one place as to certain claims of which they did not take jurisdiction, and partially in another place as to others of which they did take jurisdiction,—the two partial statements being complementary one of the other, and forming together a perfectly intelligible and complete judgment as to the whole matter.

The direct effect of the judgment as between the United States and Great Britain, is to prevent either Government, when a Belligerent, from claiming of the other, when a Neutral, "an award of compensation or computation of damages" for any losses or additional charges or "general expenses of war," which such Belligerent, in its political capacity as a nation, may suffer by reason of the want of due diligence for the prevention of violation of neutrality in the ports of such Neutral. That is to say, the parties to the Treaty of Washington are estopped from claiming compensation, one of the other, on account of the national injuries occasioned by any such breaches of neutrality, not because they are *indirect* losses,—for they are not,—but because they are *national* losses, losses of the State as such. And each of us may, in controversies on the same point with other nations, allege the *moral* authority of the Tribunal of Geneva.

But, while *national* losses incurred by the Belligerent as a State in consequence of such breaches of neutrality are not to be made the subject of "compensation or computation of damages," all private or individual losses may be, under the qualifications and limitations as to character and amount found by the Tribunal, and which will be explained in treating of that part of the Decision.

These conclusions are the inevitable result of careful comparison of the several claims with the several decisions. True it is, the *national* claims of indemnity for the cost of the pursuit of the Confederate cruisers happened to come before the Tribunal associated with strictly *private* claims, and the strictly *private* claims on account of payment of extra war premiums associated with *national* claims; but these are perfectly immaterial incidents, which do not in any way affect appreciation of the *opinions* of the Tribunal.

Another subject of reflection suggests itself, in comparing the respective decisions on national and on private losses, produced by the failure of a Neutral to maintain neutrality.

We asserted the responsibility of Great Britain for the acts of such of the Confederate cruisers as came within either of the three Rules, just as if those cruisers had been fitted out or supplied by the British Government, to the extent at least of the prizes of private property which those cruisers made. That was the *theory* of imputed responsibility. Any cruiser enabled to make prizes by the fault of the British Government was to be regarded as *pro tanto* a British cruiser, and Great Britain, in the words of the British Counter-Case, "treated [in that respect] as a virtual participant in the war." The Tribunal seems to have so held; that is, in regard to the losses of individual citizens of the United States.

Moreover, it was argued on both sides, as by common consent, that the question between the two Governments was one of war, commuted for indemnity.

"Her [Great Britain's] acts of actual or constructive complicity with the Confederates," says the American Argument, "gave to the United States the same right of war against her, as in similar circumstances she asserted against the Netherlands.

"We, the United States, holding those rights of war, have relinquished them to accept instead the Arbitration of this Tribunal. And the Arbitration substitutes correlative legal damages in the place of the right of war."

This position is clearly stated in the British Counter-Case as follows:

"Her Majesty's Government readily admits the general

"principle that, where an injury has been done by one nation "to another, a claim for some appropriate redress arises, and "that it is on all accounts desirable that this right should be "satisfied by amicable reparation instead of being enforced by "war. All civil society reposes on this principle, or on a prin-"ciple analogous to this; the society of nations, as well as that "which unites the individual members of each particular com-"monwealth."

Now the capture of private property on the seas, it can not be denied, is one of the methods of public war. Whether such capture be made by letters of marque, or by regular men-of-war, is immaterial; in either form it increases the resources of one Belligerent and it weakens those of the other; and if the Neutral fits out [or, in violation of neutral duty, suffers to be fitted out in its ports, which is the same thing] cruisers in aid of one of the Belligerents, such Neutral becomes a virtual participant in the war, not only prolonging it and augmenting its expenses, but perhaps producing decisive effects adverse to the other Belligerent. These are the national losses, or, as the British Government insists, the indirect losses, inflicted by neglect or omission to discharge the obligations of neutrality.

In deciding that such losses,—that, in general, the national charges of war,—can not by the law of nations be regarded as "good foundation for an award of compensation or computation of damages between nations," the Tribunal in effect relegated that question to the unexplored field of the discretion of sovereign States.

Claims of indemnity for the national losses growing out of a state of war being thus disposed of, we arrive at the great class of private losses, which chiefly occupied the time of the Tribunal.

DECISION AS TO PRIVATE LOSSES.

The Arbitrators, assuming that, pursuant to the command of the Treaty, they are to be governed by the three Rules, and the principles of international law not incompatible therewith, proceed to lay down the following prefatory positions, namely:

1. "The 'due diligence' referred to in the first and third of the said Rules, ought to be exercised by neutral Governments in exact proportion to the risks to which either of the Belligerents may be exposed from a failure to fulfill the obligations of neutrality on their part.

2. "The circumstances, out of which the facts constituting the subject-matter of the present controversy arose, were of a nature to call for the exercise on the part of Her Britannic Majesty's Government of all possible solicitude for the observance of the rights and the duties involved in the proclamation of neutrality issued by Her Majesty on the 13th day of May, 1861.

3. "The effects of a violation of neutrality committed by means of the construction, equipment, and armament of a vessel are not done away with by any commission which the Government of the belligerent Power benefited by the violation of neutrality may afterward have granted to that vessel; and the ultimate step, by which the offense is completed, can not be admissible as a ground for the absolution of the offender; nor can the consummation of his fraud become the means of establishing his innocence.

4. "The privilege of ex-territoriality accorded to vessels of war has been admitted into the laws of nations, not as an absolute right, but solely as a proceeding founded on the principle of courtesy and mutual deference between different nations, and therefore can never be appealed to for the protection of acts done in violation of neutrality.

5. "The absence of a previous notice can not be regarded as a failure in any consideration required by the law of nations, in those cases in which a vessel carries with it its own condemnation.

6. "In order to impart to any supplies of coal a character inconsistent with the second Rule, prohibiting the use of neutral ports or waters, as a base of naval operations for the Belligerent, it is necessary that the said supplies should be connected with special circumstances of time, of persons, or of place, which may combine to give them such character."

Keeping in view these rules of construction, the Tribunal proceeds to judge the British Government in regard to each of the Confederate cruisers before them.

As to the *Alabama*, originally "No. 290," constructed in the port of Liverpool and armed near Terceira, through the agency of the *Agrippina* and *Bahama*, dispatched from Great Britain to that end, the Tribunal decides that the British Government failed to use due diligence in the performance of its neutral obligations:

1. Because "it omitted, notwithstanding the warnings and official representations made by the diplomatic agents of the United States during the construction of the said 'No. 290,' to take in due time any effective measures of prevention, and that those orders which it did give at last, for the detention of the vessel, were issued so late that their execution was not practicable;" 2. Because, "after the escape of that vessel, the measures taken for its pursuit and arrest were so imperfect as to lead to no result, and therefore can not be considered sufficient to release Great Britain from the responsibility already incurred;" 3. Because, "in despite of the violations of the neutrality of Great Britain committed by the '290,' this same vessel, later known as the Confederate cruiser *Alabama*, was on several occasions freely admitted into the ports of Colonies of

Great Britain, instead of being proceeded against, as it ought to have been, in any and every port within British jurisdiction in which it might have been found;" 4. And because " the Government of her Britannic Majesty can not justify itself for a failure in due diligence on the plea of the insufficiency of the legal means of action which it possessed."

As to the *Florida*, originally called *Oreto*, the Tribunal decides that the British Government failed to use due diligence to fulfill its duties:

1. Because "it results from all the facts relative to the construction of the *Oreto* in the port of Liverpool, and to its issue therefrom, which facts failed to induce the Authorities in Great Britain to resort to measures adequate to prevent the violation of the neutrality of that nation, notwithstanding the warnings and repeated representations of the Agents of the United States;" 2. Because "it likewise results from all the facts relative to the stay of the *Oreto* at Nassau, to her issue from that port, to her enlistment of men, to her supplies, and to her armament with the co-operation of the British vessel *Prince Alfred* at Green Cay, that there was negligence on the part of the British Colonial Authorities;" 3. Because, " notwithstanding the violation of the neutrality of Great Britain committed by the *Oreto*, this same vessel, later known as the Confederate cruiser *Florida*, was nevertheless on several occasions freely admitted into the ports of British Colonies;" and, 4. Because "the judicial acquittal of the *Oreto* at Nassau can not relieve Great Britain from the responsibility incurred by her under the principles of international law; nor can the fact of the entry of the *Florida* into the Confederate port of Mobile, and of its stay there during four months, extinguish the responsibility previous to that time incurred by Great Britain."

As to the *Shenandoah*, originally called the *Sea King*, the Tribunal decides that the British Government is not chargeable with any failure in the use of due diligence to fulfill the duties of neutrality respect-

L

ing her during the period of time anterior to her entry into the port of Melbourne: but—

"That Great Britain has failed, by omission, to fulfill the duties prescribed by the second and third of the Rules aforesaid, in the case of this same vessel, from and after her entry into Hobson's Bay, and is therefore responsible for all acts committed by that vessel after her departure from Melbourne, on the 18th day of February, 1865."

The Tribunal further decides as to the *Tuscaloosa*, tender to the *Alabama*, and as to the *Clarence*, the *Tacony*, and the *Archer*, tenders to the *Florida:*

"That such tenders or auxiliary vessels being properly regarded as accessories, must necessarily follow the lot of their principals, and be submitted to the same decision which applies to them respectively."

As to the other vessels accused, namely, the *Retribution, Georgia, Sumter, Nashville, Tallahassee,* and *Chickamauga,* the Tribunal decided "that Great Britain has not failed, by any act or omission, to fulfill any of the duties prescribed by the three Rules of Article VI. in the Treaty of Washington, or by the principles of international law not inconsistent therewith."

Thus far the Tribunal had dealt only with the considerations of law and of fact applicable to the general question of the naked legal responsibility of Great Britain.

As preparatory to the ulterior question of the sum to be awarded to the United States by way of indemnity, the Tribunal decides; 1. "That prospective earnings can not properly be made the subject of compensation, inasmuch as they depend in their nature upon future and uncertain contingencies;" 2. "In order to arrive at an equitable compensation for the damages which have been sustained, it is necessary to set aside all double claims for the same losses, and all claims for 'gross freights' so far as they exceed 'net freights;'" 3. "It is just and reasonable to allow interest at a reasonable rate."

Finally, the Tribunal, deeming it preferable, in accordance with the spirit and the letter of the Treaty of Washington, to adopt the form of adjudication of a sum in gross rather than to refer the subject of compensation to Assessors, concludes as follows:

"The Tribunal, making use of the authority conferred upon it by Article VII. of the said Treaty, by a majority of four voices to one, awards to the United States the sum of fifteen millions five hundred thousand dollars in gold as the indemnity to be paid by Great Britain to the United States for the satisfaction of all the claims referred to the consideration of the Tribunal, conformably to the provisions contained in Article VII. of the aforesaid Treaty.

"And, in accordance with the terms of Article XI. of the said Treaty, the Tribunal declares that 'all the claims referred to in the Treaty as submitted to the Tribunal are hereby fully, perfectly, and finally settled.'

"Furthermore, it declares that each and every one of the said claims, whether the same may or may not have been presented to the notice of, or made, preferred, or laid before the Tribunal, shall henceforth be considered and treated as finally settled, barred, and inadmissible."

It deserves to be remembered that the British Arbitrator, and he alone, refused to sign the Decision. No good reason appears to justify this refusal, seeing that the signature is but authentication, and the body of the Decision sets forth all the differences of opinion existing among the Arbitrators. Thus, Mr. Adams and Mr. Stæmpfli were overruled on two questions; and yet they signed the Act. So the Vicomte d'Itajubá was overruled on the great question of the liability of Great Britain for the *Shenandoah*; and yet he signed the Act. In separating himself from his colleagues in this respect, the British Arbitrator exhibited himself as what he was, as most of his actions in the Tribunal demonstrated,—as his subsequent avowal established,—not so much a Judge, or an Arbitrator, as the volunteer and officious attorney of the British Government.

EFFECT OF THE AWARD.

In reflecting on this Award, and seeking to determine its true construction, let us see, in the first place, what it actually expresses either by inclusion or exclusion.

The Award is to the United States, in conformity with the letter of the Treaty, which has for its well-defined object to remove and adjust complaints and claims " on the part of the United States."

But the history of the Treaty and of the Arbitration shows that the United States recover, not for the benefit of the American *Government* as such, but of such individual citizens of the United States as shall appear to have suffered loss by the acts or neglects of the British Government. It is, however, not a special trust legally affected to any particular claim or claimants, but a general fund to be administered by the United States in good faith, in conformity with their own conceptions of justice and equity, within the range of the Award. If, according to any theory of distribution adopted by the United States, the sum awarded prove inadequate, we have no claim on Great Britain to supply the deficiency: on the other hand, if the Award should prove to be in excess, we are not accountable to Great Britain for any balance. On this point, precedents exist in the diplomatic history of Great Britain herself.

The Tribunal does not afford us any rules of limitation affecting the distribution of the Award, unless in the declaration that "prospective earnings," "double claims" for the same losses, and "claims for gross freights, so far as they exceed net freights," can not properly be made the subject of compensation,— that is to say, as against Great Britain.

Nor does the Tribunal define affirmatively what claims should be satisfied otherwise than in the comprehensive terms of the Award, which declares that the sum awarded is "the indemnity to be paid by Great Britain to the United States for the satisfaction of *all the claims referred to the consideration of the Tribunal,* conformably to the provisions contained in Article VII. of the aforesaid Treaty."

The Arbitrators,—be it observed,—do not say for *the satisfaction of certain specific claims among those referred to the consideration* of the Tribunal, but of "*all* the claims" so referred conformably to the provisions of the Treaty.

Now, the practical question which arises is whether the schedules of claims, which were presented to the Tribunal as documentary proofs on the part of the United States, are conclusive, either as to what they contain or what they do not contain, to establish rules of distribution under the Award.

This point is settled by what occurred in discussions before the Tribunal.

Great Britain had presented a table, composed in large part of estimates, appreciations, and arbitrary or suppositious averages: in consequence of which the United States presented other tables, to which the British Agent objected that these tables comprehended claimants, and subjects of claim, not comprised in the actual schedules filed by the United States: to which the American Agent replied by showing that the Tribunal had before it, in virtue of the Treaty, all the reclamations made by the United States in the interest of individuals injured, and comprised under the generic name of *Alabama* Claims [le tribunal reste saisi de la question de toutes les réclamations faites par les Etats-Unis dans l'intérêt des individus lésés, et comprises sous le nom générique de réclamations de *l'Alabama*].

Some discussions on the same subject afterward occurred between Mr. Stæmpfli and Sir Alexander Cockburn, which conclusively prove that the result reached did not accept as binding either the tables presented by the United States or the deductions therefrom claimed by Great Britain. The estimate of Mr. Stæmpfli seems to have been the basis of conclusion;

and that estimate is founded on dividing the difference between the American estimate of $14,437,000, and the British estimate of $7,074,000, the mean of which is $10,905,000: which mean does not in any sort represent the *actual* claims of the United States.

Indeed, one of the Arbitrators expressly declared that, in arriving at a conclusion, the Arbitrators were not to be regarded as making an assessment, or confining themselves to the schedules, estimates, or tables of either of the two Governments.

Whether the sum awarded be adequate, depends, in my opinion, on whether distribution be made among *actual losers only* and *citizens of the United States*.

ALIDITY OF THE AWARD.

The principles of the Award are in conformity with the Rules of the Treaty, which do but embody in precise language the traditional policy, inaugurated by Washington with the active support of Jefferson, professed by every successive President of the United States, and authenticated by repeated Acts of Congress.

That Great Britain loyally accepts the Award, and will in due time pay to the United States the amount awarded, it is impossible to doubt. The Queen's speech, at the opening of the present session of Parliament, not only declares the acquiescence of the British Government in the Award, but also recommends speedy payment in conformity with the tenor of the Treaty.

And while prominent members of both Houses,

such as the Earl of Derby, the Marquess of Salisbury, and Lord Cairns, in the House of Lords, and, in the House of Commons, Mr. Disraeli, Mr. Horsman, and others, spoke complainingly of the Treaty, and of the new Rules, rather than of the Award, yet Lord Granville, the Marquess of Ripon, and the Lord Chancellor, in one House, and Mr. Gladstone, Mr. Laing, Mr. Lowe, and others, in the other House, defended the whole transaction with its results, as alike beneficial to Great Britain and the United States.

Among the discontented persons is Mr. Laird, who finds himself characterized as one of those who prefer "private gain to public honor," and who seems to think that the Government of that day did not *investigate* him and his family so much as it might and should have done to the end of detecting and exposing the false pretenses with which they covered up the illegal destination of the *Alabama*. Lord Redesdale also continues to mourn over the insensibility of the British Government to his partnership argument, and refuses to be comforted, although the Government did, in fact, present the argument with all possible seriousness in the British Counter-Case and elsewhere, in season to have it distinctly responded to by the Counsel of the United States (Argument, p. 479 and *seq.*), and considered or not considered by the Tribunal.

The elaborate speeches of the Earl of Derby and Mr. Disraeli sufficiently indicate the footing on which objection to the Treaty and to the Award is to be placed in England. Little is said in criticism of the amount awarded as indemnity. Earl Granville, indeed, does not fail to remind the Earl of Derby of the admission made by the latter in the House of Commons, to the effect that the Americans were very likely to establish their claims, or some of them at least, and to get their money. This admission on the part of Lord Stanley evinced his manliness and truthfulness. Even the Chief Justice at Geneva was forced to concede the responsibility of Great Britain for the acts of the *Alabama*, and did not very skillfully escape making the same concession as to the *Florida*.

The marvel is, that Lord Russell should have so persistently refused to agree to any terms of redress, when he himself could write to Lord Lyons on the 27th of March, 1863, " that the cases of the *Alabama* and *Oreto* were a scandal, and, in some degree, a reproach to our laws." I demand of myself sometimes, in reflecting on the strange obstinacy of Lord Russell in this respect, as contrasted with the conduct of the Earl of Derby, the Earl of Clarendon, and Earl Granville, whether there be not some mystery in the matter, some undisclosed secret, some unknown moral coercion, to account for and explain the conduct of Lord Russell? The extraordinary incident of the failure of the Government to obtain from the Law Officers of the Crown any response to the call for their opinion in season to detain the *Alabama*,—which incident Sir Roundell Palmer vainly attempted to explain at Geneva,—would really tend to make one suspect that some member of the Government more powerful than himself had defeated those good intentions of Lord

Russell, with which he is credited by Mr. Adams. May it not have been, must it not have been, Lord Palmerston? Is Earl Russell solely responsible for the deplorable errors of that Administration?*

---

* I repeat, in Great Britain issue is not to be made on the pecuniary part of the Award, but on the construction of the opinions expressed and the legal conclusions arrived at by the Tribunal of Arbitration.

The opinions of *all* the Arbitrators in the case of the *Alabama*, including that of the British Arbitrator, are concurrent to the effect that, by reason of the mendacity of her builders, the Lairds, co-operating with corruption, negligence, or stupidity on the part of the Board of Customs, the British Government was made responsible for the depredations committed by her on the commerce of the United States.

But the circumstances of the actual escape of the *Alabama* reveal a singular imperfection in the administrative mechanism of the British Government.

On the 23d of July, 1862, the British Government was aroused from its indifference in regard to the equipment of the *Alabama*, by receiving from Mr. Adams, with some other papers, an opinion of a Queen's Counselor, Mr., now Sir Robert, Collier, to the effect that, if the *Alabama* were suffered to depart, the Board of Customs and the Government would incur "heavy responsibility." The case had become urgent. The *Alabama* might sail at any moment. Lord John Russell hastened to hide himself under the robes of the "Law Officers of the Crown,"—that is to say, Sir John Harding, the Queen's Advocate-General; Sir William Atherton, the Attorney-General; and Sir Roundell Palmer, the Solicitor-General.

But the oracles did not speak until the 29th of July, and then advised *detention;* in consequence of which, on *the morning of that day*, the *Alabama*, whose managers appear to have had intimate knowledge of every step taken or not taken by the Government, departed from Liverpool.

Lord John Russell, in a conference with Mr. Adams on the 31st of July, imputed this misadventure to " the sudden devel-

It deserves to be noted in this relation that although Edwards and possibly some other of the pub-

---

opment of a malady of the Queen's Advocate, Sir John D. Harding, which had utterly incapacited him for the transaction of business. This," he added, "had made it necessary *to call in other parties* [he does not say, others of the *Law Officers*], whose opinion *had been at last given* for the detention of the gun-boat."

The Counsel of the United States, in their Argument, invite attention to the unsatisfactoriness of this explanation. They found in the Documents annexed to the British Case eight opinions of the "Law Officers of the Crown," prior to that of July 29th, *all of which, except one dated June* 30*th*, are signed by Sir John Harding, and also either by Sir William Atherton or by Sir Roundell Palmer. Thereupon, we inferred that the Queen's Advocate had become sick on or before the 30th of June; and we also inferred that "it was not necessary on the 29th of July to call in new parties, but only to call upon the old." These inferences were legitimate, and were confirmed in the sequel by the highest authority.

But thereupon the British Arbitrator, after speaking of the last inference as "an ungenerous sneer," remarks:

"The unworthy insinuation here meant to be conveyed is, that Lord Russell stated that which was untrue,—an insinuation which will be treated as it deserves by every one who knows him. It is obvious that Mr. Adams must, in this particular, have misunderstood his Lordship."

The Chief Justice unconsciously admits that if Lord Russell said this, "he stated that which was untrue," and expects us to disbelieve Mr. Adams in order to shield Lord Russell.

I prefer to believe Mr. Adams. Nay, the statement imputed to Lord Russell by Mr. Adams is in substance *reaffirmed and adopted in the British Case* [p. 118].

The senseless prejudice which fills the mind of the Chief Justice in reference to the United States, their Agent, and their Counsel, is rendered the more conspicuous here by the fact that, when he threw out this "ungenerous sneer" and this "unlic officers, whose negligence or fraud has reflected so seriously on the British Government, may have been

---

worthy accusation" of his against the American Counsel, he had before him a statement on the subject, presented to the Tribunal of Arbitration by Sir Roundell Palmer, as follows :.

"Sir John Harding was ill from the latter part of June, 1862, and did not, after that time, attend to Government business. It was not, however, known, until some weeks afterward, that he was unlikely to recover; nor did the disorder undergo, till the end of July, such a development as to make the Government aware that the case was one of permanent mental alienation.

"Although, when a Law Officer was ill, he would not be troubled with ordinary business, it was quite consistent with probability and experience that, in a case of more than usual importance, it would be desired, if possible, to obtain the benefit of his opinion. Under such circumstances, the papers would naturally be sent to his private house; and, if this was done, and if he was unable to attend to them, some delay would necessarily take place before the impossibility of his attending to them was known.

"Lord Russell told Mr. Adams [July 31, 1862] that some delay had, in fact, occurred with respect to the *Alabama* in consequence of Sir John Harding's illness. He could not have made the statement, if the fact were not really so; because, whatever the fact was, it must have been, at the time, known to him. The very circumstance that Sir J. Harding had not already advised upon the case in its earlier stage might be a reason why it should be wished to obtain his opinion.

"Sir J. Harding and his wife are both [some years since] dead; so are Sir W. Atherton [the then Attorney-General] and his wife; no information, therefore, as to the circumstances which may have caused delay, with respect to the delivery at their private house, or the transmission and consideration of any papers on this subject, can now be obtained from them.

"The then Solicitor-General was Sir R. Palmer, who is able to state positively that the first time he saw or heard of the papers sent to the Law Officers [*i. e.*, all three Law Officers] on dismissed, yet it does not appear that any of the guilty parties, such as Laird, Miller, Thomas, Prioleau,

---

the 23d and 25th or 26th of July, was on the evening of Monday, the 28th of July, when he was summoned by the Attorney-General, Sir W. Atherton, to consider them in consultation, and when the advice to be given to the Government was agreed upon." Sir R. Palmer thinks it his duty to add, that "no Government ever had a more diligent, conscientious, and laborious servant than Sir W. Atherton; and that it is in the last degree unlikely that he would have been guilty of any negligence or unnecessary delay in the consideration of papers of such importance."

We thus learn that in the latter part of June, as the American Counsel had supposed, Sir John Harding was unable to attend to the business of the Government. Next, we are informed that the papers *might have* been sent to his private house, to remain there unattended to; but *it is not asserted that they were so sent in fact.* Nay, we are left to conjecture that they *might have been* sent to the house of Sir William Atherton; *but it is not asserted that they were.* Indeed, Sir Roundell Palmer speaks of "the delivery at *their* private house," meaning apparently "houses." Next, we are asked to believe that, because of the death of "Sir J. Harding and his wife," and that of "Sir W. Atherton and his wife," no means exist to explain the fatal delay in this case, by reason of which so much loss and shame have been brought on Great Britain.

Was it ever before imagined that the death of an Advocate-General or an Attorney-General, and *their wives*, should leave a Government wholly without means of knowledge on such a subject, or should be put forward to explain such delay of action on the part of Ministers?

Who carried the papers to the house either of Sir John Harding or Sir William Atherton, or both? Why did Lord Russell permit six days to elapse without inquiring for the answer to his reference when every hour was pressing for action? Who brought the papers away from the place in which they were, whether the house of Sir J. Harding, or the house of Sir or other Englishmen, whose false representations deceived the British Government, and involved Great

W. Atherton, if they ever went to either? Why were they not sent to the house of Sir Roundell Palmer? How did they ultimately get into the hands of Sir William Atherton and Sir Roundell Palmer?

Now, whatever Sir Roundell Palmer says I believe; and his declaration shows that there is no more reason to suppose the papers were sent, either to Sir J. Harding or to Sir W. Atherton, of which nothing is known, than that they were sent to Sir R. Palmer himself, to whom we know they were not sent, as he positively declares.

Observe that Sir R. Palmer takes pains to commend the diligence, conscientiousness, and industry of Sir W. Atherton, from which it is plain to infer that he never received the papers. Of course, the allusion to the death of him and his wife is as little to the purpose as that to the death of Sir J. Harding and his wife, or the insanity of Sir J. Harding.

Another observation. According to Sir Roundell Palmer's statement, there were two successive references to the Law Officers,—on the 23d and the 25th or 26th. He implies that *each* of these references *might have been* communicated to Sir J. Harding and to Sir William Atherton. He does not speak of the insane Sir J. Harding *alone*, as Lord Russell does; but is careful to make excuse in like manner for the sane Sir W. Atherton. Now, when he was called in for consultation on the evening of the 28th, did it not occur to him to inquire why these sets of papers, each one of which ought to have been communicated *to him* at their respective dates, were not so communicated? Why speculate on the effects of the insanity of Sir J. Harding or the integrity of Sir W. Atherton? Why not as well lay before us conjectural inferences founded on the diligence or uprightness of him, Sir R. Palmer? Should not the suppression of the papers as to himself have suggested to him that they had been suppressed as to Sir J. Harding and Sir W. Atherton?

We revert now to Lord Russell's statement to Mr. Adams,

Britain in this perilous controversy with the United States, have ever been punished in any way. Indict-

that the delay was caused by the insanity of Sir J. Harding, *which made it necessary to call in other parties.* What other parties? Why, forsooth, the other two "Law Officers of the Crown" disguised by Lord Russell under the designation "other parties." But Sir R. Palmer assures us that the papers [if, indeed, they were sent at all] must have been sent originally "to *the* Law Officers, *i. e., all three* Law Officers." Lord Russell therefore had no more right to impute the delay to Sir J. Harding than to Sir W. Atherton; for, even to this day, Sir R. Palmer can not say to which of the two, *if to either*, the delay is imputable. And yet Lord Russell implies that the delay was occasioned by the insanity of Sir J. Harding, while neither he nor Sir R. Palmer ventures to affirm that the papers were ever sent to Sir J. Harding.

In view of all these imperfect and irreconcilable statements, the presumption remains that some person in the Government had the means of traversing its intention, and withholding these papers from all the three Law Officers until the *Alabama* was ready to sail. I do not say Lord Russell was that person; but I think he knows who it was; and if he desires to vindicate his honor, of which he and the Chief Justice say so much, he will best do it, not by "sneers" at the American Counsel, but by disclosing the name of the person in the Foreign Office who thus betrayed and dishonored the Government.

All questions depending on this incident are now terminated. But the incident itself has permanent value as illustrating the weakness of the British Government on the side of its so-called "Law Officers,"—that is, busy members of the Bar, distracted by their private practice, but in whose opinions the Government lives and moves; who have "papers sent" to them by the Government in every great emergency, without their being actual and ever present members of the Government, like the "Law Officers" of the United States.

Here, in the United States, as in the case of the *Maury*, for ments were, indeed, found against some inferior persons, but not against the responsible authors of the loss and shame which the *Alabama* and the *Florida* brought on Great Britain. Traces occasionally appear in the journals of London of some discontent on the part of tax-payers, who are now called on to respond to the United States for the dishonorable gains of the Lairds and the Millers. Expressions of sentiment in this respect appear in the recent debates in the House of Commons. Indeed, if an account were taken of the injury inflicted on the British people by the actual losses in Confederate bonds purchased in Great Britain, and the profits lost on bonds of the United States not purchased there and sold instead in Germany; the losses on British ships and cargoes captured in attempting to run the blockade of Southern ports; the payment by the Government to the United

---

instance, "papers are presented to the Secretary of State by the British Minister on the 11th day of October, 1855, alleging unlawful equipment in violation of neutrality by that vessel; the papers are sent to the Attorney-General on the 12th, and on the same day orders are given by telegraph to embargo the vessel, and are actually executed on the 13th at New York.

Mr. Fawcett has not without reason called the attention of the House of Commons to this defect in the conduct of the law business of the British Government. The reply that the Attorney or Solicitor General should be allowed to continue in private business, in order to possess *competent knowledge* for the conduct of the business of the Government, is quite preposterous; it would be just as reasonable to insist that the Lord Chancellor or the Chief Justice of the Queen's Bench must continue at the Bar.

States of indemnity for the captures made by the *Alabama*, the *Florida*, and the *Shenandoah;* the rise in the cost of cotton and naval stores, and the consequent losses to commerce, to manufactures, and to labor, in Great Britain, occasioned by the prolongation of our Civil War: in reflecting on all this, it will be perceived that the hasty issue of the Queen's Proclamation, which gave to the Confederates a standing in Great Britain, and the means and spirit to continue hostilities, was an ill-advised measure, hardly less injurious to Great Britain than it was to the United States. These are matters which, as questions of diplomacy between the two Governments, the Treaty of Washington and the Award of the Tribunal close up; but they remain as historical facts, full of admonition to all Governments. *Discite justitiam moniti.*

FILIBUSTER OBJECTIONS.

Do the Rules, as construed by the Decision of the Treaty, disclose that due diligence, voluntary diligence, in the discharge of neutral duties, has relation to the exigency, and that the failure therein is not excusable by the insufficiency of *statute* means of action? So thought Washington and Jefferson. They acted, when no statute existed. It avails nothing to say that ours is a constitutional government, with legal forms which impede administrative action. If Congress has not imparted to the Executive adequate powers,—if, for want of such fit legislation, the Executive can not act effectively in some given cases to prevent illegal expeditions,—if, in consequence thereof, the subjects of any friendly State are injured,—if, in a word, we should be so foolish as to insist on the privilege of possessing laws designedly imperfect, and which thus favor the violation of law, and which are insufficient to enable the President to discharge the international obligations of the United States,— then it is proper that we should pay for the enjoyment of such a privilege by answering to any friendly Power for the injurious consequences of our self-imposed impotency to perform the necessary duties of an independent sovereign State.

There is no difficulty whatever in the question. If, on the one hand, in the case of war between two other Powers, the United States desire and intend to be neutral, it is to be hoped they will not suffer themselves to be misled by the interests of some shipbuilders, or the wild schemes of some band of adventurers, foreign or domestic, or even by the sentiment of sympathy for this or that foreign cause, into permitting violations of the law of the land and of the rights of other States. If, on the other hand, the United States at any time desire or intend to go to war with some foreign Power, whether for inducements of sentiment or for objects of ambition, it is to be hoped they will manfully say so, in the face of the world, and will not sneak into national hostilities by means of the expeditions or equipments of private persons, citizens or foreigners, conducting war in disguise while the Government falsely pretends to be at peace. All such "national activities,"—that is, acts of *filibusterism*,—whether fraudulently encouraged or insufficiently discouraged by any Government, are indeed fettered by the three Rules, as they were already, so far as morality or law could do it, being classed by statute with piracy, perjury, arson, murder, and other kindred "Pleas of the Crown." True, there is tendency of opinion in the United States, as there is in Great Britain, to think that all rebellion is presumptively wrong at home, and that all rebellion is presumptively right every where else; but that is a theory which has its inconveniences. In a word, there is no possible view of the subject in which *filibusterism* is not a crime and a shame, without even the mean excuse of possible but dishonorable benefits to the United States. At all times, under all administrations, private equipments in our ports, for the purpose of hostilities against any country with which we were at peace, have been treated as what they are, criminal violations of the law of the land and of the law of nations. Statesmen, jurists, and tribunals are all of accord on this point. Contracts for such equipments are "so fraught with illegality and turpitude as to be utterly null and void." ... "There can be no question of the guilt and responsibility of a Government which encourages or permits its private citizens to organize and engage in such predatory and unlawful expeditions against a State with which that Government is at peace." ... "This principle is universally acknowledged by the law of nations. It lies at the foundation of all Government. It is, however, more emphatically true in relation to citizens of the United States." Such was the doctrine of the United

States of old: such is their doctrine now, neither more nor less by reason of our negotiation with Great Britain.

SALE OF ARMS NOT AFFECTED BY THE TREATY OR THE AWARD.

Some persons have supposed that the Treaty affects the question of the sale of arms or munitions of war to a Belligerent. That is an error. Wherever, as between the parties to the Treaty, the sale of arms was lawful before, it is lawful now; wherever it is unlawful now, it was unlawful before. That is a question to which the action of the German Embassador in Great Britain during the late war between France and Germany has drawn the attention of all Europe, and which is certain to acquire importance in any future great war; but it is not touched, in fact, by the Treaty of Washington, and did not come before the Tribunal of Geneva.

QUESTION OF SUPPLIES OF COAL.

One specific objection to the Rules of the Treaty, and only one, of any apparent force, has passed under my observation, that of the Austrian statesman, Count von Beust: the suggestion, namely, as to the second Rule, *relative to coaling and refitting in neutral ports*, which, it is alleged, " gives to England, through her possession of neutral stations in all parts of the world, a palpable advantage over other States, which have not the same facilities at command."

This objection is one of apprehension, rather than

of fact. When the United States and Great Britain shall, in conformity with the Treaty, bring the new Rules to the knowledge of other maritime Powers, such Powers will of course present for consideration all proper objections or qualifications to those Rules.

Count von Beust goes on to speak of the declaration made by Austria, Prussia, and Italy in 1866, which indicates that he was considering the subject in the relation of *contraband* rather than of simple refitting in neutral ports.

But the precise question of the supply of coal in neutral ports is not prejudged by the Treaty of Washington, nor by the opinions of the Tribunal of Arbitration. The United States are quite as much interested in having access to supplies of coal "at neutral stations in all parts of the world" as Austria, or Prussia, or Italy; and we may presume that Count Sclopis did not fail to reflect on the interests of Italy in this behalf.

One of the "Considérants" of the Award had for its special object to prevent misconstruction of the second Rule. We quote it as follows:

"In order to impart to any supplies of coal a character inconsistent with the second Rule, prohibiting the use of neutral ports or waters as a base of naval operations for a Belligerent, it is necessary that the said supplies should be connected with special circumstances of time, of persons, of place, which may combine to give them such character."

Count Sclopis explains the force of the Decision as follows:

"Quant à la question de l'approvisionnement et du chargement de charbon, je ne saurais la traiter que sous le point de vue d'un cas connexe avec l'usage d'une base d'opérations navales dirigées contre l'un des Belligérants, *ou d'un cas flagrant de contrabande de guerre.* Je ne dirai pas que le simple fait d'avoir alloué une quantité de charbon plus forte que celle nécessaire aux vaisseaux pour regagner le port de leur pays le plus voisin, constitue à lui seul un grief suffisant pour donner lieu à une indemnité. Ainsi que le disait le Chancelier d'Angleterre, le 12 Juin, 1871, à la Chambre des Lords, l'Angleterre et les Etats Unis se tiennent également attachés au principe pratique qu'il n'y a pas violation du droit des gens en fournissant des armes aux Belligérants. Mais si cet excédant de proportion dans l'approvisionnement de charbon vient se joindre à d'autres circonstances qui marquent qu'on s'en est servi comme d'une veritable *res hostilis,* alors il y a infraction à la deuxième Règle de l'Article VI. du Traité. C'est dans ce sens aussi que le même Lord Chancelier expliquait dans le discours précité la portée de la dernière parte de la dite Règle."

The same point is treated by Mr. Adams as follows:

"The supply of coals to a Belligerent involves no responsibility to the Neutral, when it is made in response to a demand presented in good faith, with a single object of satisfying a legitimate purpose, openly assigned.

"On the other hand, the same supply does involve a responsibility if it shall in any way be made to appear that the concession was made, either tacitly or by agreement, with a view to promote or complete the execution of a hostile act.

"Hence I perceive no other way to determine the degree of the responsibility of a Neutral in these cases, than by an examination of the evidence to show the *intent* of the grant in any specific case. Fraud or falsehood in such a case poisons every thing it touches. Even indifference may degenerate into willful negligence, and that will impose a burden of proof to excuse it before responsibility can be relieved."

Mr. Adams, it will be noted, dwells on the question of *intent* in this matter, as he does, indeed, in each one of his opinions, to the contrary of the line of reasoning followed by the British Arbitrator.

Finally, in assenting to the Decision, the Viscount of Itajubá remarked that, "with regard to the supply of coal, he is of opinion that every Government is free to furnish to the Belligerents more or less of that article."

Thus, the tenor of the Decision of the Tribunal, and the commentaries of the Arbitrators thereon, combine to show that the second Rule can not have the effect ascribed to it by Count von Beust.

Besides which, the latter greatly errs in supposing that the numerous naval stations possessed by Great Britain in different parts of the globe give to her so much advantage to the prejudice of other maritime Powers. She pays dearly for such benefits as she herself derives from those establishments, in the cost of maintaining them, whether in peace or in war; and if, while in a state of neutrality herself, she refuses hospitality to others [and she must do it to all, if she does to one], she forces other Powers to acquire similar establishments to be conducted with equal exclusiveness, or she is constrained to incur the risk of the charge of partiality as between several Belligerents. Hence, it is not for the interest of other Powers to overstretch the responsibilities of Great Britain in this respect; and it is for her interest to deal justly and impartially with such other Powers.

Great Britain was not condemned by the Tribunal because of the supply of coals to Confederate cruisers in her Colonial ports, nor merely because those cruisers were permitted to pervert the privilege of hospitality into making a base of operations of Nassau or of Melbourne. The recognized fault in the matter of the *Shenandoah* was mainly the augmentation of her crew at Melbourne, and the addition of equipments, without which she could not have operated as a cruiser in the North Pacific. In the case of the *Alabama*, and especially that of the *Florida*, the fault was in allowing them to come and go unmolested, and even favored, in the Colonial ports, when the British Government could no longer pretend to be ignorant of their originally illegal character, nay, when it was now fully aware of what Mr. Adams calls the "continuous, persistent, willful, flagrant falsehood and perjury," and the "malignant fraud," which attended the equipment of the Confederate cruisers in Great Britain. It was this class of facts, and not any such secondary consideration as the supply of coal, which turned the scale against Great Britain in the opinions of the Arbitrators.

No: neither the Treaty of Washington, with its Rules, nor the Decision of the Tribunal of Geneva, has inaugurated any new policy of neutrality in the United States, nor created for them any rights or any duties not previously possessed by and incumbent on the Government.

WHAT THE UNITED STATES HAVE GAINED BY THE AWARD.

What, then, it may be asked, have the United States gained by the Treaty of Washington, and by the Arbitration?

We have gained the vindication of our rights as a Government; the redress of the wrong done to our citizens; the political prestige, in Europe and America, of the enforcement of our rights against the most powerful State of Christendom; the elevation of maxims of right and of justice into the judgment-seat of the world; the recognition of our theory and policy of neutrality by Great Britain; the honorable conclusion of a long-standing controversy and the extinction of a cause of war between Great Britain and the United States; and the moral authority of having accomplished these great objects without war, by peaceful means, by appeals to conscience and to reason, through the arbitrament of a high international Tribunal.

That war, the great curse and scourge of mankind, will utterly cease because of the present successful instance of international arbitration, nobody pretends. Questions of national ambition or national resentment,—conflicts of dynastic interest,—schemes of territorial aggrandizement,—nay, deeper causes, resting in superabundant population or other internal facts of *malaise*, misery and discontent,—will continue to produce wars to the end of time.

"Non, sans doute," says M. de Mazade,—speaking of the acts of the Tribunal,—"la guerre n'est point bannie de ce monde, elle n'est pas remplacée par un tribunal de conciliation faisant rentrer au fourreau les épées impatientes d'en sortir: ce n'est pas moins un événement caractéristique et heureux que le succés de ce tribunal d'équité, de cette sorte de justice internationale." . . .

We, Great Britain and the United States, have in

this matter shown that even a question affecting, or supposed to affect, national honor, may be settled by arbitration; and if we have not effected the establishment of international arbitration as the universal substitute for war, we have co-operated to prove by our example that the largest possible questions between contending Governments are susceptible of being settled by peaceful arbitration. As Lord Ripon truly says, in so doing, we have taken a great step in the direction of the dearest of all earthly blessings, the blessing of peace.

Let us hope that other nations may follow in our footsteps. Great Britain, to her honor be it said, has been true in this respect to the engagements she entered into at the Conferences of Paris. If we of the British race are more capable of reasoning in the midst of passion than others, then ours be the glory. In all this, the sacrifices of feeling have been on the side of Great Britain. We owe the acknowledgment to her, in all sincerity. Standing, as we now do, side by side, with every cloud of offense removed from between us,—two peoples, as Mr. Gladstone has well said, on whom the seal of brotherhood has been stamped by the hand of the Almighty himself,—we may proudly point in unison to the homage we have both rendered to the cause of peace and humanity in the hall of arbitration at Geneva.

CHAPTER III.

MISCELLANEOUS CLAIMS.

TREATY PROVISIONS.

The Treaty goes on to provide, in Articles XII. to XVII. inclusive, that all claims on the part of corporations, companies, or private individuals, citizens of the United States, upon the Government of Great Britain, arising out of acts committed against the persons or property of citizens of the United States, during the period between April 13, 1861, and April 9, 1865, inclusive, not being claims growing out of the acts of the vessels referred to in the previous articles of the Treaty; and all claims, with the like exception, on the part of corporations, companies, or private individuals, subjects of Great Britain, upon the Government of the United States, arising out of acts committed against the persons or property of subjects of Great Britain during the same period, shall be referred to three Commissioners to be appointed, one by each of the two Governments, and the third by the two Governments conjointly: these Commissioners to meet at Washington, there to hear, examine, and decide upon such claims as may be presented to them by either Government.

The stipulation, it will be perceived, does not cover

all existing claims of citizens or subjects of the one Government against the other, but only claims for acts committed against persons or property on either side between certain defined dates,—that is, during the pendency of actual hostilities in the United States. It is a provision, supplementary in effect to the preceding clauses of the Treaty, conceived in the apparent intention of thus closing up all subjects of contention growing out of our Civil War.

The Commission was duly organized by the appointment of Mr. Russell Gurney, Commissioner on the part of Great Britain, and Mr. James S. Frazer, on the part of the United States, and of Count Corti, Envoy Extraordinary and Minister Plenipotentiary of Italy, Commissioner named conjointly by the two Governments.

The Treaty contains detailed provisions for the prosecution of the business before the Commission, to be completed within two years from the day of their first meeting; and the contracting parties engage to consider the decision of the Commissioners absolutely final and conclusive on each claim decided by them, —to give full effect to such decision without any objection, evasion, or delay whatsoever,—and to consider every claim comprehended within the jurisdiction of the Commissioners as finally settled, barred, and thenceforth inadmissible, from and after the conclusion of the proceedings of the Commission.

The Commissioners assembled at Washington on the 26th of September, 1871, and are assiduously engaged in the determination of the claims submitted in conformity with the Treaty, having before them as Agent for the United States, Mr. Robert S. Hale; as Agent for Great Britain, Mr. Henry Howard; with Mr. James M. Carlisle as Counsel, and Mr. Thomas C. Cox, Secretary to the Commission.

The Commission will undoubtedly complete its duties within the time prescribed by the Treaty.

PRIVATE CLAIMS ON GOVERNMENTS.

The intimate relation, which exists between the different States of Christendom at the present time, has resulted in the necessity of providing special means for adjudicating the private claims of the citizens or subjects of one Government against another. It is one of the incidents of the gradual tendency of modern nations to substitute reason for force, and arbitration for war.

The subject has not yet obtained from publicists and legislators the attention which, by reason of its great practical importance, and its intrinsic interest as an element of civilization, it deserves. It may well receive consideration here, both in itself and in its relation to other congenial stipulations of the Treaty of Washington.

All the Powers of Christian Europe and America are of accord, and stipulate in their treaties of amity and commerce, to permit to one another's subjects free ingress, residence, sojourn, and traffic in their respective territories, on the same footing with the inhabitants thereof, and with subjection to the laws of the land, more or less complete, according to local regulations and to the tenor of treaties. Total exemption from the local law is maintained only by the subjects of Christian States in countries outside of Christendom.

In most of the countries of Christendom foreigners are protected in their personal rights equally with the inhabitants, and, if wronged, have access to the tribunals for redress, even against injuries by the local Government itself.

Generally, indeed, it may be said, with truth, that the rights of a foreigner are better protected than those of the inhabitants of the country itself; for, in addition to the tribunals of the country where he sojourns, the foreigner has the benefit of the Minister and Consuls of his own country.

Of this favor the foreigner has occasional need, it is true; but it is a privilege susceptible of great abuse, by reason of the extravagant pretensions occasionally made by persons who may suffer any real or apparent wrong, and who are prone to elevate trivial grievances into international questions, to the annoyance of all Governments, and to the peril of the public peace. Most of such subjects of complaint are capable of being settled by the local tribunals, and ought to be. The laws of Rome lie at the foundation of the jurisprudence of all Europe and America alike; the forms of judicial administration are substantially similar in all the States of both Continents; and in many of the cases of alleged wrong to foreigners, and of call for diplomatic intervention, the affair is one which, if at home in his own country, the party would never dream of withdrawing from the courts of law to make the alleged injury a subject of claim against his Government. And it would greatly tend to the harmony of States and the peace of the world, if treaty stipulations were entered into in order to diminish the extent and restrain the frequency of such private claims on foreign Governments.

In the present condition of things, every Government is forced by private importunity into becoming too often the mere attorney of the claims of its citizens against foreign Governments, in matters where the party aggrieved, if aggrieved, has ample means of redress before the tribunals, and where his grievance does not in the slightest degree affect the honor of his own Government.

These observations apply especially to incidents occurring in times of peace, in which times the acts of willful injury, done by any Government to foreigners sojourning under its treaty protection, are few in number compared with the injuries done to its own subjects or citizens, by any, the best administered Government either of Europe or America. On such occasions, the injured party not seldom exaggerates his case, and, by appeals to the sentiment of *citizenship* in his own country, seeks to force his Government to interpose in his behalf, so as to obtain for him summary redress by diplomatic means in disregard of the local law.

Meanwhile, in times of war, the resident or sojourning foreigner is still more solicitous to be exempt from those ordinary consequences of military operations to which the inhabitants of the country are subject, and his solicitude is in proportion to the injuries to which he is thus exposed. This fact became conspicuous in the late war between Germany and France, and led to many complaints on the part of British subjects voluntarily residing at the seat of war, which constrained Lord Granville to disabuse them of the idea that armies in the field were to fold their arms and cease to act, lest by chance they might, in the heat of action, disturb the peace of mind, or damage the property or person, of some commorant Englishman.

Incidents of this nature are most of all frequent in times of civil war, especially in those countries of Spanish America, where *militarism* prevails, and the regular march of civil institutions is interrupted by military factions headed by generals, in contention with one another, and with the constituted authorities of the Government.

For injuries thus done to its subjects, residing or sojourning in a foreign country, every Government possesses of course the right of war or of reprisals, which, in effect, is the same thing, being the adoption of force as a remedy in lieu of reason: a method of redress for private injuries, which, however common formerly, is contrary to all the prevalent notions of international justice in our day.

Hence, while it is the right and duty of every Government to interpose on proper occasion, through its Ministers or Consuls, or otherwise, on the happening of any injury to its citizens or subjects abroad, yet the recurrence to force as a means of redress is admissible only in very rare and exceptional cases of aggravated wrong committed by the authorities of the foreign Government.

The Government aggrieved in the person of its subject obtains, in many cases, the redress of the particular injury by more or less earnestness of diplomatic remonstrance.

If, however, redress be delayed for some sufficient cause to excuse the delay, and cases of alleged injury are thus accumulated, indemnity for the injuries done will be procured by diplomatic negotiation, if the injured Government be patient and persistent; for, much as there may be of evil in the world, and frequently as nations depart on occasion from the rule of right, yet, after all, the sense of justice among men and the conscience of nations prevail to such extent that, in the end, in most cases, mere appeals to reason suffice to obtain voluntary reparation at the hands of the injuring Government.

Thus, without war, and without threat of war, the United States have obtained, by treaty, payment of indemnity, for injuries to citizens of the United States, from other Governments, such as France, Denmark, the Two Sicilies, Spain, with provision for the distribution of such indemnity, among our citizens, by ourselves, through the agency of commissioners appointed under Act of Congress.

USEFULNESS OF MIXED COMMISSIONS.

In other controversies of this class between the United States and foreign Governments, where agreement as to the nature of the injury or amount of the indemnity could not be arrived at, mixed commissions have been established by treaty in numerous instances, to judge and decide the questions at issue between the two contending Governments.

On three several occasions, within a brief period, the United States and Great Britain have had recourse to the international tribunal of a mixed commission for settlement of unliquidated claims of citizens or subjects of one country against the Government of the other, namely, by the Treaty of July 26, 1853; by that of July 1, 1863; and by the present Treaty of Washington. Other examples of this occur in our earlier history. And the United States have had treaties of a similar character with the Mexican Republic, with the Republic of New Granada, with that of the United States of Colombia, and with the Republics of Costa Rica, Venezuela, and Peru.

An eminent French publicist, M. Pradier Fodéré, observes:

"L'arbitrage, très-usité dans le moyen-âge, a été presque entièrement négligé dans les temps modernes; les exemples d'arbitrage offerts et acceptés sont devenus de plus en plus rares, par l'expérience des inconvénients qui semblent être presque inséparables de ce moyen, ordinairement insuffisant par le défaut d'un pouvoir sanctionnateur. Lorsque les grandes puissances constituent un tribunal arbitral, ce n'est ordinairement que pour des objets d'intérêt secondaire."

As to the absence of any power to compel observance of the award of an international tribunal, it may suffice to say that the "pouvoir sanctionnateur" is in the treaty of arbitration, which nations are quite as likely to observe as they are to observe any other treaty. It is that question of good faith among nations upon which the peace of the world stands.

Undoubtedly, cases occur in which the international discord or debate turns on questions where the national honor or dignity is directly in play, and where the controversy becomes a matter of personal sentiment; and in such cases it may not be easy to obtain an agreement to arbitrate. Such, indeed, was the view of Earl Russell, as we have already seen, with reference to the imputed want of due diligence of the British Government in the matter of the *Alabama* and the *Florida*. But the influence of time, which softens sensibilities and resentments, and the prevalence at length of the mutual desire of peace, may overcome even the most serious apparent obstacles to friendly arbitration, as the conduct of Great Britain in expressing her regret for the incidents of which the United States complained, and in referring the whole subject to the Tribunal at Geneva, seems to demonstrate.

OTHER FORMS OF ARBITRATION.

Many instances have occurred in the present century of another form of arbitration, differing materially from mixed commissions, namely, submission to a single arbiter or tribunal, with complete authority to decide the subject of controversy.

Thus, in 1851, France and Spain referred to the arbitration of the King of the Netherlands the question of responsibility for certain prizes, an incident of the intervention of France in the affairs of Spain in the time of Ferdinand VII. In 1827, Great Britain and the United States referred a question of boundary to the King of the Netherlands. In 1843, France and England submitted a question of indemnities claimed by British subjects to the King of Prussia. In 1844, France and Mexico submitted a similar question to the Queen of Great Britain. In 1852, the United States and Portugal submitted to the Emperor of the French the question of the responsibility of Portugal for the destruction of an American letter-of-marque by the English in the port of Fayal. In 1858, the United States and Chile submitted a question of private loss to the decision of the King of the Belgians. In 1862, a difference between some English officers and local Brazilian authorities was submitted to the arbitration of the King of the Belgians by Great Britain and Brazil. In 1867, Great Britain and Portugal submitted a question of territory to the decision of the United States. In 1870, Brazil and the United States referred a question of damages to the decision of Sir Edward Thornton, the British Minister. In 1864, Great Britain and Peru submitted a question of private claims to the judgment of the Senate of the free city of Hamburg.

We shall presently have to speak of a fact of the same class in the question referred by Great Britain and the United States to the Emperor of Germany by the Treaty of Washington.

One of the earliest of our conventions of this nature was contained in the Treaty of 1818, in execution of an article of the Treaty of Ghent [1815], by which the United States and Great Britain stipulated to refer a certain question of indemnities to some friendly Sovereign or State. Afterward the Emperor of Russia was selected as such arbitrator, and rendered an award against Great Britain, in general terms, by reason of which it became necessary to provide by a second treaty [1822] for the appointment of a commissioner and arbitrator on the part of the United States, and a commissioner and arbitrator on the part of Great Britain, to assemble at Washington and assess damages under the umpirage of the Minister of the mediating Power accredited to the United States. This example is curious and instructive, seeing that the debtor Government, so to speak,—Great Britain,—in order to give effect to its engagement at Ghent entered into three successive international compacts with the United States,—one to appoint an arbiter, another to name him, and a third to give effect to his award. There could be no better illustration of the moral force of treaties of arbitration in the estimation of modern States.

TENDENCY OF REASON AND JUSTICE TO PREVAIL OVER FORCE.

These many examples, it seems to me, tend to manifest the increasing desire of modern nations to terminate all their controversies, if possible, by friendly means rather than by force. Where they can not agree between themselves, they establish a mixed commission or appoint an arbitrator or arbitrators. On such occasions the contending parties do not select an arbitrator in consideration of his being powerful, like an Emperor of the French or an Emperor of Germany, but because of confidence in the impartiality of the arbiter, as when great States refer a question to relatively feeble Sovereigns, like the King of the Netherlands or the King of the Belgians, or to the Senate of a little Republic like Hamburg, or even to five individual judges, like the Arbitrators of Geneva, or to a single person like Sir Edward Thornton. Nay, in further proof of the availableness of this method of settling national disputes, we have Great Britain and the United States, in spite of their own particular quarrel, each trusting the other in a question between either of them and another Power.

The same disposition of mind on the part of modern Governments, that is, the assumption that a selected international judge or arbitrator will decide impartially, whether he be powerful or weak, and of whatever nationality he may be, appears in the constitution of mixed commissions. Generally these commissions consist of two commissioners, one appointed by each of the respective Governments, with authority given to the commissioners to select an umpire to determine any differences which may arise between them; or sometimes the umpire is agreed on by the two Governments.

Now, in the very heat of our late controversies with Great Britain, we consented to accept the British

Minister, Sir Frederic Bruce, as umpire between us and the United States of Colombia. And at the same period of time, Great Britain accepted Mr. B. R. Curtis, of Massachusetts, as umpire under the Treaty for settling the claims of the Hudson's Bay Company against the United States. And in this case, be it remembered, the Commissioners, just men both, Sir John Rose and Mr. Alexander S. Johnson, agreed on their award without troubling Mr. Curtis.

Under the previous claims' Treaty between Great Britain and the United States, the two Governments in the first instance agreed on ex-President Van Buren as umpire, and, on his declining, they chose Mr. Bates, an American Banker residing in London.

Under the claims' Treaty between the United States and New Granada, an American, Mr. Upham, of New Hampshire, was umpire; and another American, Dr. Francis Lieber, of New York, under the recent Treaty between the United States and the Mexican Republic.

Strongest of all is the case of the Treaty between Paraguay and the United States, which submitted their controversy to an American citizen, Mr. Cave Johnson, of Tennessee, as sole arbiter, and he decided against the United States.

Is it possible to misapprehend the *moral* of such facts? In all these various aspects of the subject, do we not perceive the sense of justice tending every day to penetrate deeper and deeper into the councils of nations, and the voice of reason, of which international *law* is the expression, influencing more and more the action of Governments?

THEORY OF ARBITRATION.

Sovereign States, it has been said, should be trusted to do justice spontaneously, and without humbling themselves to be judged by an arbitrator. It might with just as good reason be said that all men should be trusted to do justice spontaneously, and without humbling themselves to be judged by a tribunal. The experience of mankind contradicts each of these propositions. Diverse views of the facts, and of the rules of right applicable to the facts, to say nothing of prejudice, passion, pride of opinion, are inseparable from human affairs, because they are conditions of the human mind, influencing the actions as well of men in political society as of individual men. Admit that in a majority of cases reason will prevail to prevent or to settle controversies between individual persons; but reason does not suffice in all cases, and it is for such exceptional cases that tribunals of justice exist, without which, in the attempt of men to right themselves, society would be dissolved into a state of anarchy and bloodshed. The considerations which recommend the establishment of tribunals having authority as such within the limits of each sovereign State, are still more cogent when applied to sovereign States themselves, which, having no common superior, must of necessity determine their differences by war, unless they accept the mediation of some friendly Power to restore concord between them, or unless they recur to arbitration, by mutual consent, in one form or another according to circumstances, as the United States and Great Britain have done by the Treaty of Washington.

So many examples of arbitration between Governments, within a recent period, contribute to prove that M. Pradier Fodéré errs in assuming that in our day "offers of arbitration made and accepted are becoming more and more rare." On the contrary, this method of terminating national differences may now be regarded as permanently fixed in the international jurisprudence of Europe and America.

WISDOM OF THE PRESENT MIXED COMMISSION.

I conclude, therefore, that the United States acted wisely in submitting the claims of British subjects to a mixed commission by the Treaty of Washington.

Some persons in the United States, with disposition to criticise the Treaty of Washington, have suggested that this Commission may result in finding a large balance of many millions due from the United States to Great Britain.

I think the supposition is altogether gratuitous, and that no such considerable balance will be found to be due. If it should be so, however, the fact will in no sort detract from the credit belonging to the Treaty. If the Government of the United States, in the course of its efforts to suppress insurrection, shall have done injury to the subjects of Great Britain for which we are justly responsible by the law of nations, it is altogether proper that we should pay whatever indemnity therefor may be found due by the judgment of a lawfully constituted international tribunal, such as the present Commission.

Citizens of the United States are not slow to invoke the intervention of their Government in behalf of any American injured in the progress of civil war in other countries, and on such occasions to talk loudly of "*outrages* to citizens:" let us do as we would be done by, and concede that Great Britain is entitled to judicial examination of the cases of her subjects alleging injury by the occurrences of civil war in the United States.

CHAPTER IV.

THE NORTHWESTERN BOUNDARY-LINE.

PROVISIONS OF THE TREATY.

THE Articles of the Treaty from XXXIV. to XLII. inclusive dispose of the long-standing dispute between the United States and Great Britain regarding the true water-line by which the Territory of Washington is separated from Vancouver's Island. The subject of the controversy, and the agreement for its termination, are set forth as follows:

"Whereas it was stipulated by Article I. of the treaty concluded at Washington on the 15th of June, 1846, between the United States and Her Britannic Majesty, that the line of boundary between the territories of the United States and those of Her Britannic Majesty, from the point on the forty-ninth parallel of north latitude up to which it had already been ascertained, should be continued westward along the said parallel of north latitude 'to the middle of the channel which separates the continent from Vancouver's Island, and thence southerly, through the middle of the said channel and of Fuca Straits, to the Pacific Ocean;' and whereas the Commissioners appointed by the high contracting Parties to determine that portion of the boundary which runs southerly through the middle of the channel aforesaid, were unable to agree upon the same; and whereas the Government of Her Britannic Majesty claims that such boundary-line should, under the terms of the treaty above recited, be run through the Rosario Straits, and the Government of the United States claims that it should be run through the Canal de Haro, it is agreed that the respective claims of the Government of the United States and of the Government of Her Britannic Majesty shall be submitted to the arbitration and award of His Majesty the Emperor of Germany, who, having regard to the above-mentioned Article of the said Treaty, shall decide thereupon, finally and without appeal, which of those claims is most in accordance with the true interpretation of the Treaty of June 15, 1846."

Subsequent articles prescribe that the question shall be discussed at Berlin by the actual diplomatic Representatives of the respective Governments, either orally or by written argument, as and when the Arbitrator shall see fit, either before the Arbitrator himself, or before a person or persons named by him for that purpose, and either in the presence or the absence of either or both Agents.

A previous arrangement in a treaty negotiated by the Earl of Clarendon and Mr. Johnson for referring the subject to the arbitration of the President of the Swiss Confederation had been rejected by the Senate of the United States, not on account of any objection to the particular arbitrator, but for other considerations.

There is good cause for the suggestion of Lord Milton that the Senate of the United States considered our "right to the disputed territory so extremely clear that it ought not to be submitted to arbitration." That, indeed, is the tenor of Senator Howard's speech on the subject, the publication of which was authorized by the Senate. Such a view of a question of right may be admissible on the part of a private individual, who, in a clear case, may prefer a suit at law in the courts of his country to arbitration; but it is wholly inapplicable to nations, which, if they can not agree and will not arbitrate, have no resource left save war.

But this was not the only consideration which induced the Senate to refuse its assent to that treaty. There were objections to the *form* of submission.

HISTORY OF THE QUESTION.

The controversy to which these treaties refer is one of the leavings of the last war between the United States and Great Britain, and has its roots far back in the circumstances of the primitive colonization of North America by Europeans.

When the Kings of the little island of Britain, in virtue of some of their subjects having coasted along a part of the Atlantic shores of America, assumed to concede to the Colonies of Massachusetts and Virginia grants of territory extending by parallels of latitude westward to the Pacific Ocean, and covering the unexplored immensity of the Continent, and on the premises' of sovereignty and jurisdiction as good as their title to the manor of East Greenwich in Kent,—it was only men's universal ignorance of geography which saved the act from the imputation of wild extravagance.

But such grants, and the pretensions on which they were founded, were the logical consequence of the theories of colonization and conquest pursued in the New World by Spain, Portugal, and France, as well as England, and formed the basis of the power of Great Britain in North America, and eventually of that of the United States. It was the assumption that discovery by any European State, followed by occupation on the sea-coast, carried the possessions of such State indefinitely landward until they met the possessions of some other European State.

At the same time, France had entered into America by the waters of the St. Lawrence, had ascended that river to the Lakes, had then descended by the Mississippi to the site of the future New Orleans, and had thus laid the foundation of a title not only to the explored territories watered by the St. Lawrence or in front of it on the sea-coast, but also to undefined, because unknown, regions beyond the Mississippi.

Hence arose the first great questions of boundary in North America, those between England, France, and Spain, which were settled by the Peace of Utrecht. France retained possession of the territories on the St. Lawrence and the Mississippi; whilst England retained her country of Hudson's Bay and her Provinces on the Atlantic coast, and acquired Nova Scotia and Newfoundland. [Treaty of Utrecht, March 31–April 11, 1713.]

Subsequently, the fortunes of war made England mistress of the Canadian and coast establishments of France, leaving to the latter only the territory beyond the Mississippi. [Treaty of Fontainebleau, Nov. 3, 1762, and Treaty of Paris, Feb. 10, 1763.]

Meanwhile, Spain continued, with but brief interruption, in undisputed sovereignty of the two Floridas, and of the vast provinces of New Spain, of undefined extension west and north toward the Pacific.

Thus, when the Thirteen Colonies obtained independence, and treated for the partition between them and Great Britain of the British empire in America, each took the part of which they respectively held constructive jurisdiction, according to its recognized limits in time of peace,—that is to say, Great Britain retained for herself the territories which she had conquered from France, and relinquished to the Thirteen Colonies all the territory which she had theretofore claimed as hers against France by title of colonization and possession.

The new Republic thus became the sovereign of a magnificent territory regarded in the comparison with European standards of magnitude, and also of intrinsic value and resources unsurpassed by the possessions of any European State.

But, even with such limits, we felt cribbed and confined from the first: for the statesmen of the United States had clear perception not only of what we possessed as territory, but also of what we needed to possess in order to be a first-rate Power in America.

We found ourselves blocked in on the North by the British possessions, which also overshadowed us on the East, and which were at that time of sufficient relative strength to constitute an object of solicitude to us so long as they remained in the hands of Great Britain.

Westward, we were hemmed in along the Mississippi by the French, who also held the mouths of that river, and barred us from access to the sea in that direction.

On the South, Spain shut us up on the side of the Gulf of Mexico.

It was impossible in this state of things that the United States could attain the development to which, in other respects, they had the right to aspire, by reason of the fertility of their soil, their numerous rivers, and their commanding position in the temperate zone of America.

But the cession of Louisiana to the United States by the voluntary act of France,—the most splendid concession ever made by one nation to another,—produced a revolution in the condition of America. We thus acquired territory of indefinite limits westward, with such limits on the south as the pretensions of Spain would allow, and with limits north only where superior claim of right on the part of Great Britain intervened, namely, the parallel of forty-nine degrees established between France and Great Britain by the Treaty of Utrecht.

President Jefferson lost no time in asserting the rights of the United States in the interior of the Union, and at the same time acquiring knowledge of the country by means of the celebrated expedition of Lewis and Clark. Theretofore the only knowledge we possessed of the great chain of the Rocky Mountains, and of the country or even the name of the country of Oregon beyond, was founded on the narration of Jonathan Carver, or other information derived from the Indians.

We were thus enabled to comprehend the relation of Louisiana to the shores of the Pacific, and to see that the River Columbia, first entered by Captain Robert Gray of the American ship *Columbia*, of Boston, in 1792, and named by him, and afterward by the English explorer, Captain Vancouver, was "the great river of the West," the Oregon of Carver.

That coast had already been explored with more or less of diligence by Spanish navigators, fitted out by the Viceroys of New Spain, who gave to many of the islands, straits, and channels the names they still retain; and Spain, if any Power anterior to the United States, had title by discovery in those parts of America.

But the earliest settlement on that coast was the factory of Astoria at the mouth of the River Columbia, established by John Jacob Astor.

Then came the war between the United States and Great Britain: the first effect of which, as to the present question, was the military occupation of Astoria and of the country on the banks of the Columbia by British forces: subsequently to which, on the conclusion of peace, although Astoria was surrendered to us in obedience to the stipulations of the Treaty of Ghent, yet Great Britain set up claim to the valley of the Columbia as against the United States, and, indeed, to all the country intervening between the actual occupations of Spain to the south in California, and those of Russia to the north in Sitka.

Claims of Great Britain in this quarter, with but weak foundation, had already been asserted against Spain to the south of the River Columbia.

Controversy on the subject between the United

States and Great Britain was suspended by the Treaty of October 20, 1818. By that treaty it was stipulated that from the Lake of the Woods to the "Stony Mountains," the line of demarkation between the possessions of the two countries in America should be the forty-ninth parallel of latitude westward to the Stony Mountains.

The United States might well have insisted on proceeding due west from the most northwestern point of the Lake of the Woods, the terminal point in that direction of the Treaty of Independence, which is nearer the parallel of 50°; but, in early unsuccessful negotiations on this subject under President Jefferson, we had agreed to adopt the 49th parallel, and that agreement was renewed by the Treaty of 1818, in obedience to the assumption that this line had been established by the Treaty of Utrecht.*

---

* The "Treaty of Peace and Amity" between France and England contains the following provision [Art. X.]:

"Quant aux limites entre la Baie de Hudson et les lieux appartenans à la France, on est convenu réciproquement qu'il sera nommé incessamment des Commissaires, qui les détermineront dans le terme d'un an: ... les mêmes Commissaires auront le pouvoir de régler pareillement les limites entre les autres colonies Françaises et Britanniques dans ce pays-là."—Dumont, t. viii., pt. 1, p. 332–338.

Mr. Bancroft, misled by Mr. Greenhow, says of this article:

"On the Gulf of Mexico, it is certain that France claimed to the Del Norte. At the northwest, where its collision would have been with the possessions of the Company of Hudson's Bay, no treaty, no commission, appears to have fixed its limits."—Bancroft's *History*, vol. iii., p. 343.

It was further provided by the same treaty that the country claimed by either Party westward of the Stony Mountains, with its harbors, bays, and creeks, and the navigation of all rivers within the same, should be free and open for the term of ten years to the vessels, citizens, and subjects of the two Powers: it being understood that this agreement should be without prejudice to any exclusive claim of either, or to the claim of any other Power.

This treaty, which regulated the occupation of Oregon for so many years, although apparently equal on its face, was very unequal, as we shall see, in fact, by reason of the whole country being immediately overrun and almost exclusively occupied by the Hudson's Bay Company.

But the pretensions of the United States received notable reinforcement through the Treaty between

---

Mr. Madison had previously said, as if not perfectly certain of the fact:

" *There is reason to believe* that the boundary between Louisiana and the British territories north of it was actually fixed by Commissioners appointed under the Treaty of Utrecht, and that the boundary was to run from the Lake of the Woods westwardly on latitude 49°."—*American State Papers, Foreign Affairs*, vol. iii., p. 90.

The point was settled, however, by inquiries made by Mr. Monroe at London. He says:

" Commissaries were accordingly appointed who executed the stipulations of the treaty in establishing the boundaries of Canada and Louisiana by a line beginning on the Atlantic at a cape or promontory in 58° 30′ north latitude; thence southwestwardly to the Lake Mistosin; thence farther southwest to the latitude 49° north, and along that line indefinitely." — *American State Papers, Foreign Affairs*, vol. iii., p. 97.

Spain and the United States of February 22, 1819, by which the former ceded to the latter the two Floridas, carrying our territory down to the Gulf of Mexico, and by which also a line of demarkation was run between the territories of the respective Parties west of the Mississippi. This line, commencing on the Gulf of Mexico at the mouth of the River Sabine, proceeds by that river, the Red River, and the Arkansas, to its source in latitude 42° north; "and thence by that parallel of latitude to the South Sea." And Spain expressly ceded to the United States all her "rights, claims, and pretensions to any territories east and north of the said line, as thus defined and described by the treaty." To the rights, claims, and pretensions of the United States on the northwest coast we could now add those of Spain.

But another pretender to rights on that coast now appeared in the person of Russia, whose actual occupation came down to the parallel of 54° 40'; and thereupon it was agreed between Russia and the United States by Treaty of April 17, 1824, that the latter would not permit any settlement by its citizens on the coast or islands north of that degree, and that no subjects of the former should be permitted to settle on the coast or islands south of the same degree. Neither Government, however, undertook to make any cession to the other. Nor was the country south of the line described as a territory or possession of the United States.

During the next year, Russia and Great Britain concluded a treaty for the demarkation of the limits between them in the same quarter by a line which, beginning in 54° 40' at the southernmost point of Prince of Wales Island, was made to run obliquely to strike the main-land at latitude 56°, and then to proceed parallel to the windings of the coast at the distance of not exceeding ten marine leagues therefrom along the summit of the coast mountains to its intersection with the 141st degree of longitude at Mount St. Elias, and thence due north along that meridian to the Frozen Ocean.

It has been too much the practice of British navigators and British map-makers to affix English names to places previously visited and named by other Europeans, and to found thereon claims of discovery. English names are scattered along the coast of Russian America,—such as Cook's Inlet, Prince William Sound, King George III. Archipelago, Prince of Wales Archipelago;—but no British claims of prior exploration could prevail here against the claims of possession as well as discovery presented by Russia.

In this treaty, each Government speaks as the proprietor and sovereign of the respective territories; and it is this treaty which defines and marks out the Territory of Alaska, as now held by the United States under recent cession from Russia.

In this condition stood the title for more than twenty years: the United States claiming from the latitude of 42° to that of 54° 40', in virtue, first, of their own discoveries and settlement, and of the right of the extension of Louisiana until it should reach the ocean or some recognized possession of another Power, and, secondly, in virtue of the discoveries and rights of extension of Spain; and Great Britain claiming in virtue of discovery and possession, and of rights of extension of her actual admitted possessions in America.

Thus we arrive at the question of what her actual admitted possessions were: which is the key to the Treaty of June 15, 1846, the interpretation of which was referred to the Emperor of Germany.

On the restoration of Charles II., projects of colonization and of remote commercial or speculative enterprises, which had been suspended in England during the Civil War, began to be resumed with new zeal, comprehending as well the East as the West Indies.

Among the great territorial charters of that day, one of the most interesting is that of the Hudson's Bay Company, by which the King granted to sundry persons, including the Prince Rupert, the Duke of Albemarle, the Earl of Craven, Lord Arlington, Lord Ashley, Sir John Robinson, Sir Edward Hungerford, and others [in part, it will be perceived, the same persons who obtained a grant of the two Carolinas],

"The sole trade and commerce of all those seas, straits, bays, rivers, lakes, creeks, and sounds, in whatsoever latitude they shall be, that lie within the entrance of the straits commonly called Hudson's Straits, together with all the lands and territories upon the countries, coasts, and confines of the seas, bays, lakes, rivers, creeks, and sounds aforesaid, that are not already actually possessed by or granted to any of our subjects, or possessed by the subjects of any other Christian Prince or State, with the fishing of all sorts of fish, whales, sturgeons, and all other royal fishes in the seas, bays, inlets, and rivers within the premises and the fish therein taken, together with the royalty of the sea upon the coasts within the limits aforesaid, and all mines royal, as well discovered as not discovered, of gold, silver, gems, and precious stones, to be found or discovered within the territories, limits, and places aforesaid, and that the said land be from henceforth reckoned and reputed as one of our Plantations or Colonies in America, called 'Rupert's Land.'"

This concession was induced, as the preamble of the charter sets forth, by the reason that the parties

"Have, at their own great cost and charges, undertaken an expedition for Hudson's Bay, in the *northwest* part of America, for the discovery of a new passage to the South Sea, and for the finding some trade for furs, minerals, and other considerable commodities, and by such their undertaking have already made such discoveries as do encourage them to proceed farther in pursuance of their said designs, by means whereof there may probably arise very great advantage to us and our Kingdom."

The Company's Charter, in common with others of that period, conveyed to them the right to hold the territory granted with all rights and jurisdictions appertaining thereto, as of the manor of East Greenwich in Kent; the Company became lords and proprietors of Rupert's Land on condition of a yearly payment to the Crown of "two elks and two black beavers;" and no legal impediment existed to the establishment on Hudson's Bay of a local political government such as existed in Massachusetts or Virginia; but, in reflecting on the slow growth of the British Colonies in the more temperate latitudes of North America, it will be readily seen that no colonization could be effected on the frozen and desolate shores of Hudson's Bay. In effect, the Company very soon resolved itself into a mere commercial undertaking for trade in the furs of the vast region in the space between Canada or New France and the Arctic Sea, inhabited only by wandering bands of Indians.

When the great Succession War broke out, involving all Europe, it could not fail to reach America; for the possessions of three of the four principal Powers engaged,—France, Great Britain, and Spain, —occupied alternate points on the coast of the Atlantic. The French, of course, endeavored to avail themselves of the opportunity to drive out or to weaken the English on both sides of them, and especially in Rupert's Land, which they invaded and partly conquered, but restored by the subsequent Treaty of Utrecht.

After this time, the Company, safe in its arctic solitudes, prospered without check for a century, filling Rupert's Land with forts and factories, and engrossing the fur trade of North America.

Thereupon a rival Company entered the field, under the auspices of the Province of Canada, founding its enterprise on the assertion that Rupert's Land had only a limited extension south and west, to cover no more than the water-shed terminating at Hudson's Bay, with no rights or jurisdiction southward and westward to the great Lakes and the Rocky Mountains.

After a long and violent controversy, the Northwest Fur Company was by agreement of parties merged to the Hudson's Bay Company.

The combined influence of the parties interested in

the aggregate Company enabled it to obtain for a term of years, first in 1821, and afterward in 1838, exclusive right to trade with the Indians in certain parts of North America not belonging to Prince Rupert's Land.

The region of country thus opened by license exclusively to the Hudson's Bay Company is described in the license of 1838 as follows:

"The exclusive privilege of trading with the Indians in all such parts of North America to the northward and to the westward of the lands and territories belonging to the United States of America as should not form part of any of our provinces in North America, or of any lands or territories belonging to the said United States of America, or to any European Government, State, or Power."

In so far as these licenses affected only the region west and south of Hudson's Bay depending on Lake Winnipeg, Lake Athabasca, the two Slave Lakes, and other lands east of the Rocky Mountains, they did not concern the United States.

But in so far as they affected the region west of the Rocky Mountains, such a license is in plain violation of treaties with the United States. The Queen of England could give a license in that region to the Hudson's Bay Company *exclusive of all other Englishmen;* but she could not give any to exclude citizens of the United States. That, indeed, the grant does not profess to do; but, in effect, it did that and more; for in the hands of the Company it was "a charter of licensed usurpation and pillage in the whole of the described region of North America." The Company established forts or posts at every eligible or strategic point between the mountains and the shores of the Pacific; their servants killed the fur-bearing animals; they cut and exported the timber; and, by means of its wealth and organization, the Company monopolized the commerce and the resources substantially to the exclusion for a long time of the people of the United States.

But at length some settlements of Americans had been commenced in Oregon; and the attention of Congress was called to the usurpations of the Hudson's Bay Company by Mr. Benton, Mr. Linn, and the writer of these pages: in consequence of which steps were taken to put an end to the joint occupation of Oregon. In fact, the Company had now set up the most extravagant pretensions, exaggerating a mere license to trade into a grant of proprietorship to the whole of the immense region south and west of Rupert's Land, to the dissatisfaction of the people of Canada as well as of the United States. For it was the interest of the Company to retain the whole country occupied by them in the condition of a mere hunting-field, and quite uninhabited except by vassal Indians: while the Canadians desired that it should be opened to colonization, so as to add to the material resources and political force of the Canadian Provinces. Parliamentary inquiry into the rights of the Company was instituted; it was imperatively instructed by Sir Edward Bulwer Lytton [afterward Lord Lytton], Colonial Minister [whose dispatches show that he was not less eminent as a statesman than as a poet and a novelist], to desist from all general pretensions of proprietorship founded upon license to trade; its license was revoked; it was compelled to yield up Oregon to the United States; and it was half-persuaded and half-constrained to sell its chartered rights to the Canadian Dominion, and to shrink into comparative insignificance in America.

When the Government of the United States entered into negotiations with Great Britain for terminating the joint occupation of Oregon, the machinations of the Hudson's Bay Company were the great disturbing fact which for a long time prevented the conclusion of a treaty and its due execution.

Meanwhile the two Governments, after extraordinary contention, at length arrived at a settlement of another boundary question, which had remained open ever since the Treaty of Independence, namely, the boundary-line on the northeast between the British possessions and the United States [Treaty of November 20, 1842].

The duration of the Treaty of 1818 was limited to ten years. As the expiration of this time approached, the American Government offered to settle the question of Oregon by extending the line of 49° to the Pacific Ocean, and announced this as "our ultimatum." The British Government objected that this line would cut off the southern part of Vancouver's Island. We replied by proposing to yield this part for an equivalent. But it was for the interest of the Hudson's Bay Company, which was in practical possession of the whole country, to defeat this attempt at settlement, and it was defeated, and the United States reluctantly consented to the prolongation of the nominal joint occupation.

But the discussions in Congress heretofore mentioned, and the disposition of Americans to settle in Oregon, had, in 1842, rendered the joint occupation intolerable to the people of the United States, and the negotiation for settlement was renewed on the premises of the 49th parallel. The baleful influence of the Hudson's Bay Company caused the negotiation to drag on for the period of four years; when the Treaty of 1846 was at length concluded, yielding to Great Britain the southernmost extremity of Vancouver's Island.

It was the question of *Vancouver's Island* which chiefly occupied the succeeding negotiators. To run the line on the 49th parallel to the sea, and "thence by the Canal de Haro and Straits of Fuca to the ocean," was Lord Aberdeen's proposition to Mr. McLane. And the same understanding of the question,—that is, to concede to Great Britain "Vancouver's Island, and nothing else south of latitude 49°,"—pervades the dispatches and debates on both sides. And on such premises, notwithstanding much opposition in Congress and out of it, the United States acceded to these terms as a measure of peace and of conciliation toward Great Britain.

But strife was unexpectedly renewed two years afterward by Lord Palmerston, or by Lord John Russell, who had succeeded as Premier to Sir Robert Peel, and their action has kept up dispute on the subject between the two Governments for more than twenty years solely on account of pretensions which ought not to have been raised, and the injustice of which has now at length been demonstrated by the Award of the Emperor of Germany. If this Award be unwelcome to the people of Great Britain, no feeling of unkindness in that respect should be attached by them to the United States. The Canal de Haro was undoubtedly intended by the negotiators of the Treaty of 1846 as the water-boundary in that quarter: that intention accords with the obvious and only reasonable signification of the language of the treaty.

THE AWARD.

This conclusion is clearly and conclusively proved in the Memorial presented in the name of the American Government to the German Emperor by the American Plenipotentiary and Agent, Mr. George Bancroft, and in his Reply to the Case of Great Britain.

Mr. Bancroft was pre-eminently fitted for the performance of this duty. Possessing intellectual qualities of a high order, and particular personal estimation at the Court of Berlin, he enjoyed the advantage of having been a member of the Cabinet under whose auspices the Treaty of 1846 was negotiated,—of subsequently representing his Government at the Court of St. James at the time when the present controversy commenced,—and of being thoroughly master of all the older diplomatic incidents of the question by his studies as the historian of the United States. Of the value of all these qualifications to his Government on the present occasion, we have the proof in two most complete and most convincing arguments which he addressed to the Emperor of Germany.

The Agent on the part of Great Britain was Admiral James C. Prevost, who had been the Commissioner of his Government, in association with Mr. Archibald Campbell, Commissioner of the United States, for determining and marking the line of boundary prescribed by the treaty, and who, of course, possessed all the special knowledge requisite for the preparation of any possible argument in support of the pretensions of Great Britain.

The Emperor, it appears, referred the arguments on both sides to three experts, Dr. Grimm, Dr. Kiepert, and Dr. Goldschmidt, personages among the most eminent of his subjects in jurisprudence and in science, upon whose report he decided on the 21st of October, 1872, in the terms of the reference, that the claim of the United States to have the line drawn through the Canal de Haro is most in accordance with the true interpretation of the treaty concluded on the 15th of June, 1846, between Great Britain and the United States.

"This Award," says the President's Message of December 2, 1872, "confirms the United States in their claim to the important archipelago of islands lying between the continent and Vancouver's Island, which for more than twenty-six years [ever since the ratification of the treaty] Great Britain had contested, and leaves us, *for the first time in the history of the United States as a nation*, without a question of disputed boundary between our territory and the possessions of Great Britain on this continent."

In recent debates in the House of Lords, the Earl of Lauderdale criticised the Treaty of Washington in severe terms, partly on the assumption that the United States have in reserve new claims respecting the northwestern boundary-line. He is mistaken. Nothing remains but questions of hydrography for Commissioners to determine, which there is no difficulty in doing; and arrangements have already been made by the two Governments for the appointment and organization of the requisite Commission.

In conclusion, let me say that Great Britain has no cause to regret the adverse conclusion of this controversy. The conditions of the Treaty of 1846 involved positive *concession* on the part of the United States, if not as to the general line, yet in giving up the whole of the Island of Vancouver without any compensation. We certainly did not mean at the same time to give up the important island of San Juan, and various other islands intervening between that and the main-land, which would have been the effect of admitting the Straits of Rosario as the water-boundary. We knew that prior to and during the negotiations the Canal de Haro was expressly mentioned and always understood as the true channel, corresponding to the desire of the British Government to secure Vancouver's Island.

To Great Britain it can be of no possible consequence which of the lines of boundary should be established. What possessions remain to her on the northwest coast of America, Vancouver's Island and British Columbia can not ever be of special importance to her either as a military post or as a colony. Nor can they be of any *military* advantage to the Canadian Dominion, and may, on the contrary, constitute in her hands a temptation to needless expense in fortifications, notwithstanding which, owing to the remoteness of those countries by land and their inaccessibility to her by sea, the Dominion would find them quite untenable in the presence of the powerful American States on the shores of the Pacific Ocean.

To the United States, on the other hand, it is important to have had the question decided in our favor. We are now a real power on the Pacific coast, which Great Britain is not and can not be. Holding the Territory of Alaska to the north of the British possessions, the Territory of Washington, the State of Oregon, and the great and rich State of California ceded to us by the Mexican Republic, with the growing States and Territories on their rear, it would have been to us intolerable to be excluded from the great channel between Vancouver's Island and the mainland, or to traverse it only under the guns of British fortresses on that island. Such a settlement would have had in it the germs of war: the present affords assurance of stable peace.

Happily the United States and Great Britain are now delivered from the complications in their relations occasioned by the exorbitant power of the Hudson's Bay Company. By other provisions of the same Treaty of 1846, the United States had made to Great

Britain the concession of recognizing certain pretensions of that Company in Oregon and Washington, founded on mere encroachment, and, in order to be relieved of these pretensions, paying to the Company a small sum in satisfaction of its claims, about one tenth of what was demanded for it in the name of the British Government.

Lord Milton expresses the opinion that "On a *just and equitable* solution of the so-called San Juan Water-boundary Question depends the future, not only of British Columbia, but also of the entire British possessions in North America." By "just and equitable solution" he means, of course, decision in favor of Great Britain. If the premises are correct, then the consequences are a fact accomplished. But he overestimates the value of the Archipelago of San Juan to Great Britain. His opinion assumes what is impossible, the acquisition of considerable intrinsic strength on the part of British Columbia, sustained by railroad connection with the Provinces of Ontario and Quebec. But what would avail, in a military point of view, a railroad running through a thousand miles of comparatively uninhabited country within easy reach at every point to the armies of the United States? I think the *future* of the British possessions in North America depends on a different order of facts, of which something will be said in another chapter in speaking of the commercial relations of the United States and the Canadian Dominion.

P

CHAPTER V.

THE FISHERIES.

HISTORY OF THE QUESTION.

THE TREATY OF INDEPENDENCE was, I repeat, a virtual partition of the British Empire in America between the Metropolis and the Thirteen United Colonies. It was not a treaty founded on *military* possession: for the Colonies had no such possession save along the coast of the Atlantic Ocean, and Great Britain occupied several posts north and west of the Ohio and on the Great Lakes. The theory of the treaty was to recognize the Colonies as sovereign according to their political limits as fixed by charter and by the public law of England.

In conformity with this theory, the treaty stipulates that the United States shall continue in the enjoyment of the coast fisheries, as follows:

"Article III. It is agreed that the people of the United States shall continue to enjoy unmolested the right to take fish of every kind on the Grand Bank, and on all the other banks of Newfoundland; also in the Gulf of St. Lawrence, and at all other places in the sea where the inhabitants of both countries used at any time heretofore to fish; and also that the inhabitants of the United States shall have liberty to take fish of every kind on such part of the coast of Newfoundland as British fishermen shall use [but not to dry or cure the same on that island]; and also on the coasts, bays, and creeks of all other of His Britannic Majesty's dominions in America; and that the American fishermen shall have liberty to dry and cure fish in any of the unsettled bays, harbors, and creeks of Nova Scotia, Magdalen Islands, and Labrador, so long as the same shall remain unsettled; but so soon as the same or either of them shall be settled, it shall not be lawful for the said fishermen to dry or cure fish at the said settlement, without a previous agreement for that purpose with the inhabitants, proprietors, or possessors of the ground."

Notwithstanding the absolute terms of this treaty in regard to the question of peace, there survived on both sides so much of irritation, and so many points of mutual relation remained uncertain, that the treaty was in some respects little more than a truce. We had special cause to complain of the persistent occupation of northwestern posts by Great Britain, and its effect on the Indians within our lines. On the other hand, to say nothing of minor matters, when the wars of the French Revolution commenced, and the French Republic undertook to use our ports as the base of naval operations against Great Britain, the latter Power took umbrage of course; and it was only the firm attachment of President Washington to peace, which prevented these difficulties from fatally embroiling the two countries, and which led to the conclusion of the Treaty of December 19, 1794, as the similar spirit of President Grant led to the conclusion of the Treaty of Washington.

During the next ten years, the United States labored to maintain their neutrality in the presence of the universal war by land and sea which raged between the great European Powers. Both France and England gave to us good cause of rupture; we barely escaped war with France in 1798; we were forced into war with England in 1812; and in the course of all these events the hand of the Government was restrained, if not paralyzed, by the factious force of *sympathies* in the United States, on the one side for France and on the other for England. Hence, alike in the *quasi* war with the former, and the declared war with the latter, the results as to the United States were uncertain, imperfect, trivial even, compared with the great objects which might have been accomplished by united counsels.

On the side of France, however, it must be admitted that our disposition to avoid pushing matters to extremities contributed to gain for us the immense benefit of the acquisition of Louisiana.

Afterward, although the Berlin and Milan Decrees of France and the Orders in Council of Great Britain constituted each alike good cause of war with either, yet the United States held back at vast sacrifice, until continued assertion of the right to impress seamen on board of our merchant ships, and, indeed, to visit our ships-of-war, and other exaggerations of belligerent right, forced us into war with Great Britain.

The treaty by which that war was concluded is one of the most unsatisfactory in the annals of the United States. It was absolutely silent in regard to all the subjects of controversy which had occasioned the war. Nothing is said of the belligerent encroachments of Great Britain on the neutral rights of the United States, nothing of maritime search, nothing of the impressment of real or pretended British subjects on board ships of the United States. And it left room, by its silence, for Great Britain to raise question of our right to participate in the coast fisheries, which question, although dealt with from time to time in successive treaties, has more than once seriously endangered the peace of the two Governments.

Does war have the effect of annulling all existing treaties? A general answer to this question is given by one of the most authoritative of modern publicists [Calvo] as follows:

"If the treaty of peace modifies anterior treaties, or expressly declares the renewal of them, the dispositions of the treaty of peace are thereafter to constitute the law; but if no particular mention is made in this respect, the anterior treaties must necessarily continue to have full force and effect. In order that they should be deemed definitively abrogated, it would be requisite that they shall not only be suspended by the war but annulled in fact, as in the case of treaties of alliance of which the *raison d'être* ceases at the end of the war: it would be requisite, indeed, that their contents should be incompatible with the stipulations of the treaty of peace, which occurs, for example, in what regards ancient treaties relative to the delimitation of frontiers between two States."

The Supreme Court of the United States lays down the law as follows:

"We think that treaties stipulating for *permanent rights* and general arrangements, and professing to aim at perpetuity, and to deal with the case of war as well as of peace, do not cease on the occurrence of war, but are, at most, *only suspended* while it lasts; and unless they are waived by the parties, or new and repugnant stipulations are made, *they revive* in their operations at the return of peace."

Such has been the received doctrine in the United

States, to the effect that war does not, as an absolute, universal rule, abrogate existing treaties, regardless of their tenor and particular contents; and it is the only doctrine compatible with reason, justice, common, sense, and the diplomatic history of Europe.

But the British Government, in the celebrated dispatch to Mr. Adams of October 30, 1815, signed by Lord Bathurst, and understood to be the composition of Mr. Canning, declared the position of Great Britain to be: "She knows no exception to the rule that all treaties are put an end to by a subsequent war between the same parties." This proposition, in its absoluteness of expression, if it is intended as an assertion of any established practice of nations, or any recognized doctrine of the law of nations, is unfounded and unauthorized. Many treaties are made precisely for the case of war, and only become efficacious in virtue of the existence of war. The assertion of Lord Bathurst is altogether too broad, as Dr. Bluntschli demonstrates.

Nevertheless, acting on such extreme premises, Great Britain pretended that our rights of fishery had been abrogated by the war, and were not revived by peace; and that this effect was the true interpretation of the omission to mention the subject in the Treaty of Ghent.

The Commissioners of the United States who negotiated the Treaty of Ghent were men of unquestionable patriotism and of the highest character and intelligence: it would be out of place here to reopen the dispute as to certain special causes of the failure of the Commissioners to secure in that treaty recognition of the fishery rights of the United States. But it is due to the memory of the American Commissioners, and especially to Mr. Gallatin, Mr. Adams, and Mr. Bayard, to say that, in all the negotiation at Ghent, they and their associates were hampered by the discouraged state of mind of the American Government, embarrassed, as it was, by political difficulties at home, and alarmed, if not terrified, by the triumph of Great Britain in Spain and France, and the total overthrow of Napoleon, which seemed to leave the British Government free to dispatch overwhelming forces of sea and land against the United States.

The autumn subsequent to those events was the darkest period in the history of the country. Nothing but the shock produced by the great change in the whole face of affairs in Europe could have extorted from the American Government those final instructions to our Commissioners, which authorized them to agree to the *status quo ante bellum* as the basis of negotiation,—which spoke of our right to the fisheries, and of our foreign commerce, in equivocal terms,—and which, indeed, left the Commissioners free to conclude such a treaty as their own judgment should approve under existing circumstances, provided only they saved the rights of the United States as an independent nation.

How different might and would have been those instructions, had the Government but struggled on a little longer against the adverse circumstances of the hour! Courage and procrastination would have made us masters of the situation, and enabled us to dictate terms to Great Britain.

Remember that the Treaty of Ghent was signed on the 24th of December, 1814, and that the disastrous defeat of the British forces attacking New Orleans occurred a fortnight afterward, on the 8th of January, 1815. This event, if the negotiation at Ghent had remained open, could not but have strengthened the American Government; and, two months later, all the difficulties in its path would have been removed by the landing of Napoleon at Golf Jouan [March 1, 1815] and the renewal of the war in Europe.

But the pretension of Great Britain, that the war had abrogated any part of the Treaty of Independence, was evidently untenable; and the justice of the cause of the United States was so manifest that, after three .or four years of discussion, the British Government agreed to the express recognition of our fishery rights as follows [Treaty of October 20, 1818]:

"Whereas differences have arisen respecting the liberty claimed by the United States, for the inhabitants thereof, to take, dry, and cure fish on certain coasts, bays, harbors, and creeks of His Britannic Majesty's dominions in America, it is agreed between the high contracting parties that the inhabitants of the said United States shall have, forever, in common with the subjects of His Britannic Majesty, the liberty to take fish of every kind on that part of the southern coast of Newfoundland which extends from Cape Ray to the Rameau Islands, on the western and northern coast of Newfoundland from the said Cape Ray to the Quirpon Islands, on the shores of the Magdalen Islands, and also on the coasts, bays, harbors, and creeks from Mount Joly, on the southern coast of Labrador, to and through the Straits of Belleisle, and thence northwardly indefinitely along the coast, without prejudice, however, to any of the exclusive rights of the Hudson's Bay Company. And that the American fishermen shall also have liberty, forever, to dry and cure fish in any of the unsettled bays, harbors, and creeks of the southern part of the coast of Newfoundland, hereabove described, and of the coast of Labrador; but so soon as the same, or any portion thereof, shall be settled, it shall not be lawful for the said fishermen to dry or cure fish at such portion so settled, without previous agreement for such purpose with the inhabitants, proprietors, or possessors of the ground. And the United States hereby renounce, forever, any liberty heretofore enjoyed or claimed by the inhabitants thereof to take, dry, or cure fish on or within three marine miles of any of the coasts, bays, creeks, or harbors of His Britannic Majesty's dominions in America, not included within the abovementioned limits: Provided, however, that the American fishermen shall be permitted to enter such bays or harbors for the purpose of shelter and of repairing damages therein, of purchasing wood, and of obtaining water, and for no other purpose whatever. But they shall be under such restrictions as may be necessary to prevent their taking, drying, or curing fish therein, or in any other manner whatever abusing the privileges hereby reserved to them."

In virtue of these treaty provisions, citizens of the United States continued to fish on the coasts of the British Provinces without interruption for some twenty years, when question was raised as to their right to fish *within* the bays or indents of the coast, in consequence of an opinion of the Law Officers of the Crown that the expression "three marine miles of any of the coasts, bays, creeks, or harbors," within which citizens of the United States were excluded from any right of fishing on the coast of British America, intends miles "to be measured from the headlands, or extreme points of land next the sea or the coast, or of the entrance of bays or indents of the coast," and that, consequently, American fishermen had no right to enter bays, there to take fish, although the fishing might be at a greater distance than three miles from the shore of the bay.

This opinion, be it observed, makes no distinction between close bays and open ones, large indents of the coast and small ones, and, if carried into effect by the British Government, would exclude citizens of the United States from a large part of the productive fishing-grounds on the coast of British America.

Now, strange to say, this opinion of the Law Officers of the Crown is based on a mere blunder of theirs, or, to say the least, on a fiction, or a bald interpolation.

After stating their conclusion, they assign, as the sole reason of it:

"As [that is, because] we are of opinion that the term 'headland' is used in the treaty to express the part of the land we have before mentioned, including the interior of the bays and the indents of the coasts."

It is not true that "the term 'headland' is used in the treaty to express the part of the land we have before mentioned."

Neither the term "headland" nor any word of similar signification is to be found in the treaty. The Law Officers of the Crown undertook to construe the treaty without reading it, and by this presumptuous carelessness caused the British Government to initiate a series of measures of a semi-hostile character, which came very near producing another war between Great Britain and the United States.

It may be quite admissible for the British Government, as they are accustomed to do, to throw off all their responsibilities on the "Law Officers of the Crown," when the question is one of mere domestic relation; but it is dangerous for that Government to do so in matters affecting other Governments.

We have already had occasion to comment on the very extraordinary circumstances attending the failure of the Law Officers of the Crown to report upon the case of the *Alabama*, and its disastrous influence on the conduct of the Government.

As to the opinion of the "Law Officers of the Crown" in construction of the fishery clauses of the treaty of 1818, it is difficult to say which produced the more amusement or amazement in the United States, the fact that the "Law Officers" should interpolate a phrase into the treaty in order to give to their opinion its sole foundation to stand upon, or that the British Government should placidly accept such fallacious and baseless reasoning without challenge, and proceed in obedience to it to enter into hostile maritime operations, and hurry on to the verge of war against the United States.

After much agitation and discussion, however, the question was settled for the time being by articles of the Treaty of September 9, 1854, commonly called the Reciprocity Treaty, as follows:

"Article I. It is agreed by the high contracting Parties that, in addition to the liberty secured to the United States fishermen by the above-mentioned Convention of October 20, 1818, of taking, curing, and drying fish on certain coasts of the British North American Colonies therein defined, the inhabitants of the United States shall have, in common with the subjects of Her Britannic Majesty, the liberty to take fish of every kind, except shell-fish, on the sea-coasts and shores, and in the bays, harbors, and creeks of Canada, New Brunswick, Nova Scotia, Prince Edward's Island, and of the several islands thereunto adjacent [and, by another article, Newfoundland], without being restricted to any distance from the shore, with permission to land upon the coasts and shores of those Colonies and the islands thereof, and also upon the Magdalen Islands, for the purpose of drying their nets and curing their fish; provided that, in so doing, they do not interfere with the rights of private property, or with British fishermen in the peaceable use of any part of the same coast in their occupancy for the same purpose.

"It is understood that the above-mentioned liberty applies solely to the sea-fishery, and that the salmon and shad fisheries, and all fisheries in rivers and the mouths of rivers, are hereby reserved exclusively for British fishermen."

Similar provision was made in Article II., with like exception, for the admission of British subjects to take fish on a part of the sea-coasts and shores of the United States.

It was further agreed that Commissioners should be appointed, who shall

"Examine the coasts of the North American provinces and of the United States embraced within the provisions of the first and second articles of this treaty, and shall designate the places reserved by the said articles from the common right of fishing therein."

But these provisions were temporary only, being subject to be terminated on a year's notice, after the expiration of ten years, and the treaty was in fact denounced on the 17th of March, 1865, and expired on the 17th of March, 1866.

In truth, the United States had purchased the fishery provisions of this treaty by other provisions to the effect that certain enumerated articles of the growth and produce of the British Colonies of Canada, New Brunswick, Nova Scotia, Prince Edward's Island, and Newfoundland, or of the United States, should be "admitted into each country respectively free of duty."

But the *reciprocity* here was nearly nominal, the great benefits of the provision inuring to the British Colonies. The fisheries had come to be the incident of a larger question, namely, that of the terms of commercial intercourse between the United States and the British Colonies in North America.

Dissatisfaction in the United States with this state of things led to the denouncement of the treaty, and to the revival of a controversy between the two Governments regarding the fisheries: which controversy was terminated by the Treaty of Washington.

PROVISIONS OF THE TREATY OF WASHINGTON.

By Articles XVIII., XIX., and XX., the fishery stipulations of the Treaty of September 9, 1854, are in substance revived, with further provision for the appointment of a Commission to settle any outstanding question as to the "places" of fishery reserved by either Government.

It is further agreed that fish-oil and fish of all kinds, except fish of the inland lakes and of the rivers falling into them, and except fish preserved in oil, being the produce of the fisheries of the United States, or of the Dominion of Canada, or of Prince Edward's Island, shall be admitted in each country respectively free of duty.

Then follows:

"Article XXII. Inasmuch as it is asserted by the Government of Her Britannic Majesty that the privileges accorded to the citizens of the United States under Article XVIII. of this Treaty are of greater value than those accorded by Articles XIX. and XXI. of this Treaty to the subjects of Her Britannic Majesty, and this assertion is not admitted by the Government of the United States, it is further agreed that Commissioners shall be appointed to determine, having regard to the privileges accorded by the United States to the subjects of Her Britannic Majesty, as stated in Articles XIX. and XXI. of this Treaty, the amount of any compensation which, in their opinion, ought to be paid by the Government of the United States to the Government of Her Britannic Majesty in return for the privileges accorded to the citizens of the United States under Article XVIII. of this Treaty; and that any sum of money which the said Commissioners may so award shall be paid by the United States Government, in a gross sum, within twelve months after such Award shall have been given."

The Commissioners referred to in this article are to be appointed, one by each of the two Governments, and the third by the two Governments conjointly, or, in case of disagreement between them, by the Minister at London of the Emperor of Austria and Hungary. The Commission is to sit at Halifax, in the Province of Nova Scotia.

With this provision ends the list of *Governments* concerned in this truly international Treaty, which, in the interests of peace, engages the co-operation of eight sovereign States, namely, Italy, Switzerland, Brazil, Sweden and Norway, Spain, Austria and Hungary, Great Britain, and the United States.

PROBABLE AMOUNT OF INDEMNITY.

The peculiarity of the arrangement, we see, is that the United States are to make compensation to Great Britain for any excess in *value* of the privileges of fishery accorded to the United States above those accorded to Great Britain. One party asserts, the other denies, such excess of value.

This question involves examination of facts, but it also suggests inquiry of right.

What are the privileges which the United States acquire under Article XVIII. of the Treaty of Washington? Certainly not any which they possessed already.

Now, in virtue of subsisting stipulations of the Treaty of 1818, we possessed the recognized right of fishery along the coasts, and in the bays, harbors, and creeks of British North America, subject, in so far as regards the present question, only to the renunciation which we made in that treaty of the liberty previously enjoyed or claimed, to take, dry, or cure fish on or *within three marine miles* of the coasts, bays, creeks, or harbors of *certain defined parts* of the shores of British America. The Treaty of Washington removes this limitation. Hereafter we are to fish on the sea-coasts and shores, and in the bays, harbors, and creeks, previously subject to limitation of three marine miles, "without being restricted to any distance from the shore." But we are not required to pay for any relinquishment on the part of Great Britain of the fictitious claim founded on the erroneous opinion of the Law Officers of the Crown, which, on the false assumption that "headlands" are mentioned in the Treaty of 1818, extends an imaginary line seaward three marine miles from each cape of bays and indents of the coast, joins the extremities of those two lines by a straight line, and then requires our fishermen to keep outside of this connecting line. Deluded by that opinion, the British Government, indeed, absurdly undertook to exclude us by force from the Bay of Fundy, but failed to maintain its pretension in that respect.

What we purchase is the right to enter and fish within the three marine miles of the *shores at the bottom of* certain *bays, harbors, and creeks* (from which alone we were excluded by the Treaty of 1818), disregarding wholly the opinion of the Law Officers of the Crown. Looking at the clause under consideration, in this its only proper light, it is plain that it can not impose any serious charge on the United States.

CHAPTER VI.

COMMERCIAL INTERCOURSE AND TRANSPORTATION.

TREATY PROVISIONS.

SUNDRY stipulations of the Treaty which relate to rights of navigation, and of transport by land or water, —to concessions of commercial intercourse and transit,—or to the free interchange of objects of production,—are divisible into, first, permanent provisions, and, secondly, temporary provisions.

1. Of permanent provisions we have the following:

[a] Great Britain engages that the navigation of the River St. Lawrence, ascending and descending, from the point where it ceases to form the boundary between the two countries, shall forever remain free and open for the purpose of commerce to the citizens of the United States [Art. XXVI.].

The United States engage that the Rivers Yukon, Porcupine, and Stikine, in Alaska, ascending and descending from, to, and into the sea, shall forever remain free and open for the purpose of commerce to the subjects of Great Britain [Art. XXVI.].

Rights of local police and regulation are reserved by each Government.

[b] The United States engage that the subjects

of Great Britain shall enjoy the use of the St. Clair Flats' Canal on terms of equality with the inhabitants of the United States [Art. XXVII.].

[c] The United States engage to urge on the State Governments, and Great Britain engages to urge on the Dominion of Canada, to secure each to the subjects or citizens of the other the use on equal terms of the several canals connected with the lakes or rivers traversed by or contiguous to the boundary-line between the possessions of the high contracting Parties [Art. XXVII.].

All these are provisions which bring the United States and the Dominion of Canada into fixed relations independent of and superior to all questions of *Governments*.

2. Of temporary provisions we have the following:

[a] The navigation of Lake Michigan is declared free and open for the purposes of commerce to the subjects of Great Britain [Art. XXVIII.].

[b] Goods, wares, and merchandise arriving at the ports of New York, Boston, Portland, or such other ports as the President may designate, and destined for the British possessions in North America, may be entered at the proper custom-house without payment of duties, and conveyed in transit through the territory of the United States [Art. XXIX.].

And, in like manner, goods, wares, and merchandise arriving at any of the ports of the British possessions in North America, and destined for the United States, may be entered at the proper custom-house, and conveyed in transit without the payment of duties through the said possessions; and goods, wares, and merchandise may be conveyed in transit without payment of duties, from the United States through the said possessions to other places in the United States, or for export from ports in the said possessions [Art. XXIX.].

All these rights of transit are, of course, subject to such regulations for the protection of the revenue as the respective Governments may prescribe.

[c] Great Britain engages to urge on the Dominion of Canada and the Province of New Brunswick that no export duty or other duty shall be levied on timber cut in that part of the American territory in the State of Maine watered by the River St. John and its tributaries, and floated down that river to the sea, when the same is shipped to the United States from the Province of New Brunswick.

[d] Subjects of Great Britain may carry in British vessels, without payment of duty, goods, wares, or merchandise from one port or place within the territory of the United States upon the St. Lawrence, the Great Lakes, and the rivers connecting the same, to another port or place within the territory of the United States, provided that a portion of such transportation is made through the Dominion of Canada by land carriage and in bond [Art. XXX.].

Citizens of the United States may carry in United States vessels goods, wares, or merchandise from one port or place within the British possessions in North America to another port or place within the said possessions, provided that a portion of such transportation is made through the territory of the United States by land carriage and in bond [Art. XXX.].

The United States engage not to impose any export duties on goods, wares, or merchandise carried under this article through the territory of the United States; and Great Britain engages to urge the Dominion of Canada and the other British Colonies not to impose any export duty on goods, wares, or merchandise carried under this article.

It being understood that these respective rights of transit are to be regulated by the two Governments; and that on the part of the United States the right of transit will be suspended unless the Dominion of Canada should establish the exemption from export duties required, and unless the Dominion shall open its canals on equal terms to citizens of the United States, and unless the Dominion and the Province of New Brunswick shall free from all duties the timber cut on the St. John in the State of Maine and exported to the United States [Arts. XXX. and XXXI.].

All the provisions of the Treaty from Articles XVIII. to XXI. inclusive, and Article XXX.,—that is to say, the articles regarding the fisheries and reciprocal right of transit,—are to take effect so soon as the laws required to carry them into operation shall have been passed by the Parliament of Great Britain, by that of Canada, and by the Legislature of Prince Edward's Island, on the one hand, and by the Congress of the United States on the other.

Such assent having been given, such articles shall remain in force for the period of ten years from the date at which they may come into operation, and further until the expiration of two years after either of the Parties shall have given to the other notice of its desire to terminate the same: which either may give at the end of the said ten years or at any time afterward [Art. XXXIII.].

Temporary as these provisions are, or at least terminable at the will of either Party, they are equitable in themselves, and advantageous both to the United States and the Canadian Dominion; and, like the permanent provisions of the Treaty explained in this chapter, they tend to draw the two countries closer and closer together.

The germ of the Treaty of Washington, it is to be remembered, was the suggestion of the British Government through Sir John Rose, a former Canadian Minister, whose proposal related only to pending questions affecting the British possessions in North America, not Great Britain herself.

What these questions were we partly understand by the stipulations of the Treaty, the whole of which, except those growing out of incidents of the late Civil War, are of interest to Canada, including the maritime Provinces, primarily if not exclusively, although requiring to be treated in the name of Great Britain.

To the arrangements actually made, Canada would have preferred, of course, revival of the Elgin-Marcy Reciprocity Treaty, involving the admission into each country, free of duty, of numerous articles, being the growth and produce of the British Colonies or of the United States. It was the desire of Canada to have provision made for alleged claims on account of the acts of the Fenians. But the United States would not listen to either of these propositions: so that the Dominion had opportunity to allege that she was sacrificed to the Metropolis, and thus to obtain, by way of compensation, the guaranty on the part of the Imperial Government of a large loan for the construction of the proposed trans-continental railway from the Great Lakes to the Pacific Ocean.

In some respects, the arrangements we have been considering resemble those of the Reciprocity Treaty; but they are much more comprehensive, and they are better in other respects.

We have placed the question of the fisheries on an independent footing. If the American fisheries are of inferior value to the British,—which we do not concede,—then we are to pay the difference. But the fishery question is no more to be employed by the Dominion of Canada, as it has been heretofore, either as a menace or as a lure, in the hope of thus inducing the United States to revive the Reciprocity Treaty.

Apart from other new provisions in the Treaty of Washington of less moment, there is the all-important one, stipulating for reciprocal right of commercial transit for subjects of Great Britain through the United States, and for citizens of the United States through the Dominion: in view of which Sir John Macdonald has no cause to regret his participation in the negotiation of the Treaty.

Sir Stafford Northcote, in the late debate on the Queen's speech, repels with force and truth the suggestion of Lord Bury that the Treaty of Washington is unjust to Canada. He shows, on the contrary, that the Treaty is beneficial and acceptable to the Dominion, specifying particulars, and citing the approbatory votes of the legislative assemblies of the Canadian and maritime Provinces.

But the United States will never make another treaty of reciprocal free importation, without including manufactures and various other objects of the production of the United States not comprehended in the schedule of the Elgin-Marcy Treaty. In fine, Canada must expect nothing of this nature short of a true *zollverein* involving serious modifications of the commercial relations of Canada to Great Britain.

RELATION OF THE BRITISH PROVINCES TO THE UNITED STATES.

The Dominion of Canada is one of those " Possessions," as they are entitled, of Great Britain in America, which, like Jamaica and other West India Islands, have ceased to be of any economic value to her save as markets,—which in that respect would be of almost as much value to her in a state of independence, —which she has invited and encouraged to assume the forms of semi-independent parliamentary government,—which, on the whole, are at all times a charge to her rather than a profit, even in time of peace,— which would be a burden and a source of embarrassment rather than a force in time of war,—and which, therefore, she has come to regard, not with complete carelessness perhaps, but with sentiments of kindliness and good-will, rather than of the jealous tenaciousness of sovereign power. When the Dominion shall express desire to put on the dignity of a sovereign State, she will not encounter any obstacles on the part of the Metropolis.

In regard to the Dominion of Canada, as to the Colonies of Australasia, the power of the Metropolis appears there chiefly in the person of the Governor, and in the occasional annulment of laws of the local legislatures deemed incompatible with those of the Empire. On the other hand, the Colonies, which have necessary relations of their own with neighboring Governments, as in the case of Canada relatively to the United States, can not treat thereon themselves, as their interests require they should, but must act through the intervention of the Metropolis, which, in this respect, may have other interests of its own superior and perhaps injurious to those of the Colonies.

Meanwhile the Dominion has now to provide for the cost of her own military defense, and that, not against any enemies of her own, but against possible enemies of the Mother Country. The complications of European or of Asiatic politics may thus envelop the Dominion in disaster, for causes wholly foreign to her, as much so as if she were a sovereign State. In such an emergency, the Dominion would be tempted to assume an attitude of neutrality, if not of independence.

All these considerations show how slender is the tie which attaches the Dominion to Great Britain.

The entire history of all European Colonies in America proves that the sentiment of *nationality*, that is, of attachment to the Mother Country, is very weak, and readily yields place to other sentiments of ambition, interest, or passion, so as to produce feelings of hostility between the inhabitants of the Metropolis and those of the Colonies more intense than such as exist between either of them and the inhabitants of other countries. This fact is particularly remarkable in the incidents of revolution in Spanish America, example of which we have now before the eyes in the insurrection which rages in Cuba. But the same fact appears distinctly in the past history of British America. And there is no reason to suppose that the sentiment of mere *loyalty*, that is, political attachment to the Mother Country, is any more strong at present in the Dominion of Canada than it formerly was in the British Colonies now constituting the United States.

M. H. Blerzy, in a very instructive essay on the Colonies of the British Empire, discussing the question whether the English beyond sea are likely to remain attached to England by recollections of family or of country, observes with great truth that "the very aptitude for colonization of which the English are so proud could not exist without implying a certain *insouciance* of family on their part and disdain of their native country."

How true is this remark! It is illustrated by contrasting the devoted attachment of the French to France, who in our day send so few colonists to

America, and those chiefly Basques, while hundreds of thousands annually emigrate from Great Britain.

Loyal Canadians, that is, loyal to Great Britain, must of necessity take into account this fact, which is of the very essence of British colonization in America. They are also compelled to regard another serious fact of the same order of ideas, namely, the continual emigration from Canada to the United States, not only on the part of recent immigrants from Great Britain, but,—which is more noticeable as a sign of the times,—the emigration of old Canadians, natives of the soil, in spite of all the efforts of the Government to check and discourage it.

On the other hand, the history of all European colonization shows that a time comes when the Mother Country grows more or less indifferent to the fate of her Colonies, which time appears to have arrived in Great Britain as respects the Dominion.

When Canada complains [without cause] that her wishes have been disregarded and her interests prejudiced by the stipulations of the Treaty of Washington, the great organ of opinion in England replies:

"From this day forth look after your own business yourselves: you are big enough, you are strong enough, you are intelligent enough, and, if there were any deficiency in either of these points, it would be supplied by the education of self-reliance. We are both now in a false position, and the time has arrived when we should be relieved from it. *Take up your freedom: your days of apprenticeship are over.*"

Instances might be cited of the expression of similar ideas in Parliament.

Loyalists in Canada must remember another thing. Montesquieu, with the singular penetration which distinguished him, perceives that England imparts to her Colonies "la forme de son Government," by means of which "on verroit se former de grands peuples dans les forêts mêmes qu'elle enverroit habiter." But the parliamentary form of Government, which has contributed so greatly to the growth and strength of British Colonies, gave to them facilities of successful rebellion,—that is, of separation from the Metropolis,—which no other form of government could impart, and the absence of which in Spanish America [and now in Cuba] has done so much to impede and obstruct their separation from Spain. We had experience of this in our Revolution, where each of the Colonies had a governmental organization so complete that, in order to be independent *de facto*, it needed only to *ship off* the British Governor. The same fact was apparent in our Secession War, as M. de Tocqueville had predicted. And, at this time, the Dominion of Canada needs only to substitute for a British Governor one of her own choice to become a sovereign State organized as completely as Great Britain herself.

There is another class of considerations of great importance.

War between the United States and Great Britain is now a contingency almost inadmissible as supposition, and so, of course, is war between the United

States and Canada, a possession of Great Britain. Nevertheless, the capability of a country to maintain itself by force, if need be, is one of the elements of its political life, and therefore can not be overlooked in considering the condition of the Dominion of Canada.

In regard to Canada the inquiry is the more important, seeing that military force depends in part on geographical facts, which, in her case, equally as to peace or war, and for the same reasons, place her at disadvantage on the side of the United States.

The British possessions in North America, beginning with Newfoundland on the Atlantic Ocean, and ending with Queen Charlotte's Island on the Pacific, extend across the continent in its broadest part, a distance of 80° of longitude, but in a high latitude, occupying the whole of the country north of the territory of the United States. The space thus described looks large on the map; but the greater part of it is beyond the limit of the growth of trees, and much of the residue is too cold to constitute a chosen residence for Europeans.

In a word, the Dominion stretches along thousands of miles, without capability of extension on the one side, where it meets the frozen north, or on the other, where it is stopped by the United States. As a country, it resembles a mathematical line, having length without breadth.

Meanwhile, owing to their internal position, their northern latitude, and the geographical configuration of the whole country, the two great Provinces of Ontario and Quebec have no access to the sea in the long winter, save through the United States.

Thus, if it be possible to conceive of two countries, which would appear to be naturally destined to constitute one Government, they are the United States and the British Provinces, to the special advantage of the latter rather than the former.

We therefore can afford to wait. We have nothing to apprehend from the Dominion Pacific Railway: if constructed, it will not relieve Ontario and Quebec from their *transit* dependence on the United States. We welcome every sign of prosperity in the Dominion. With the natural limitations to her growth, and the restricted capacity of her home or foreign markets, her prosperity will never be sufficient to prevent her landowners and her merchants from looking wistfully toward the more progressive population and the more capacious markets of the United States. Her conspicuous public men may be sincerely loyal to the British Crown; many of the best men of Massachusetts, New York, and Virginia were so at the opening of the American Revolution; but neither in French Canada, nor in British Canada, nor in the maritime Provinces, do any forces of sentiment or of interest exist adequate to withstand those potent natural and moral causes, or to arrest that fatal march of events, which have rendered nearly all the rest of America independent of Europe, and can not fail, sooner or later, to reach the same consummation in the Dominion of Canada.

The spirit of independence is a rising tide, in Canada as elsewhere in America, which you see in its results, if not in its progress. It is like the advancement of the sun in the sky, imperceptible as movement, but plain as to stages and ultimate destination. It is not an effect actively produced by the United States. It is an event which we would not precipitate by violence if we could, and which we scarcely venture to say we wish for, lest in so doing we should possibly wound respectable susceptibilities; but which we nevertheless expect to hail some day with hearty gratulation, as an event auspicious alike to the Dominion and to the United States.

If Lord Milton's appreciation of the course of events be correct,—and no person has written more intelligently or forcibly on the *British* side of these questions than he,—the consummation is close at hand. Arguing from the British stand-point of the San Juan Question, he says:

"If Great Britain retains the Island of San Juan and the smaller islands of the archipelago lying west of the compromise channel proposed by Lord Russell, together with Patos Island and the Sucia group, she will preserve her power upon the Pacific, and will not in any way interfere with or menace the harbors or seas which appertain to the United States. If, on the other hand, these islands should become United States territory, the highway from the British possessions on the mainland will be commanded by, and be at the mercy of that Power. . . .

"Such a condition of affairs must inevitably force British Columbia into the United States federation; and the valuable district of the Saskatchewan . . . must, *ex necessitate rei*, follow the fortunes of British Columbia. Canada, excluded from the Pacific, and shut in on two sides by United States territory, must eventually follow the same course."

In contemplation of these results, it is difficult to see how any American should fail on reflection to approve the Treaty of Washington.

"Two rival Powers," says Prêvost Paradol, "but which are but one at the point of view of race, of language, of customs, and of laws, predominate on this planet outside of Europe. . . . Destiny has pronounced; and two parts of the world at least, America and Oceanica, belong without remedy to the British race. . . . But the actual ascendancy of that race is but a feeble image of what a near future reserves to it."

The time is not remote when the United States and the Dominion of Canada will be associated in these great destinies, whether in close alliance or in more intimate union, it matters little: when "America," like "Italy," shall cease to be a mere geographical denomination, and will comprehend, in a mighty and proud Republic, the whole combined British race of North America.

But, glorious as such a consummation would be, I would not have it to be save with the cordial concurrence of the people of the Dominion, and the contented acquiescence at least of Great Britain. There is many a page of superlative triumph in the annals of the British Isles,—that England, Scotland, and Ireland of which we in the New World once were,— but not one of her days of victory can equal in lustre that of the day when Great Britain, not less proud of us, "the fairest of her daughters," than of herself, shall extend the right hand of welcome and affection to *United* America.

APPENDIX.

TREATY BETWEEN THE UNITED STATES AND GREAT BRITAIN.

Concluded May 8, 1871; Ratifications Exchanged June 17, 1871; Proclaimed July 4, 1871.

BY THE PRESIDENT OF THE UNITED STATES OF AMERICA.

A PROCLAMATION.

Whereas a Treaty, between the United States of America and Her Majesty the Queen of the United Kingdom of Great Britain and Ireland, concerning the settlement of all causes of difference between the two countries, was concluded and signed at Washington by the High Commissioners and Plenipotentiaries of the respective Governments on the eighth day of May last; which Treaty is, word for word, as follows:

The United States of America and Her Britannic Majesty, being desirous to provide for an amicable settlement of all causes of difference between the two countries, have for that purpose appointed their respective Plenipotentiaries, that is to say: the President of the United States has appointed, on the part of the United States, as Commissioners in a Joint High Commission and Plenipotentiaries, Hamilton Fish, Secretary of State; Robert Cumming Schenck, Envoy Extraordinary and Minister Plenipotentiary to Great Britain; Samuel Nelson, an Associate Justice of the Supreme Court of the United States; Ebenezer Rockwood Hoar, of Massachusetts; and George Henry Williams, of Oregon; and Her Britannic Majesty, on her part, has appointed as her High Commissioners and Plenipotentiaries, the Right Honorable George Frederick Samuel, Earl de Grey and Earl of Ripon, Viscount Goderich, Baron Grantham, a Baronet, a Peer of the United Kingdom, Lord President of Her Majesty's Most Honorable Privy Council, Knight of the Most Noble Order of the Garter, etc., etc.; the Right Honorable Sir Stafford Henry Northcote, Baronet, one of Her Majesty's Most Honorable Privy Council, a Member of Parliament, a Companion of the Most Honorable Order of the Bath, etc., etc.; Sir Edward Thornton, Knight Commander of the Most Honorable Order of the Bath, Her Majesty's Envoy Extraordinary and Minister Plenipotentiary to the United States of America; Sir John Alexander Macdonald, Knight Commander of the Most Honorable Order of the Bath, a member of Her Majesty's Privy Council for Canada, and Minister of Justice and Attorney-General of Her Majesty's Dominion of Canada; and Mountague Bernard, Esquire, Chichele Professor of International Law in the University of Oxford.

And the said Plenipotentiaries, after having exchanged their full powers, which were found to be in due and proper form, have agreed to and concluded the following articles:

Article I.

Whereas differences have arisen between the Government of the United States and the Government of Her Britannic Majesty, and still exist, growing out of the acts committed by the several vessels which have given rise to the claims generically known as the "*Alabama* Claims:"

And whereas Her Britannic Majesty has authorized her High Commissioners and Plenipotentiaries to express, in a friendly spirit, the regret felt by Her Majesty's Government for the escape, under whatever circumstances, of the *Alabama* and other vessels from British ports, and for the depredations committed by those vessels:

Now, in order to remove and adjust all complaints and claims on the part of the United States, and to provide for the speedy settlement of such claims, which are not admitted by Her Britannic Majesty's Government, the High Contracting Parties agree that all the said claims, growing out of acts committed by the aforesaid vessels and generically known as the "*Alabama* Claims," shall be referred to a Tribunal of Arbitration to be composed of five Arbitrators, to be appointed in the following manner, that is to say: One shall be named by the President of the United States; one shall be named by Her Britannic Majesty; His Majesty the King of Italy shall be requested to name one; the President of the Swiss Confederation shall be requested to name one; and His Majesty the Emperor of Brazil shall be requested to name one.

In case of the death, absence, or incapacity to serve of any or either of the said Arbitrators, or, in the event of either of the said Arbitrators omitting or declining or ceasing to act as such, the President of the United States, or Her Britannic Majesty, or His Majesty the King of Italy, or the President of the Swiss Confederation, or His Majesty the Emperor of Brazil, as the case may be, may forthwith name another person to act as Arbitrator in the place and stead of the Arbitrator originally named by such Head of a State.

And in the event of the refusal or omission for two months after receipt of the request from either of the High Contracting Parties of His Majesty the King of Italy, or the President of the Swiss Confederation, or His Majesty the Emperor of Brazil, to name an Arbitrator either to fill the original appointment or in the place of one who may have died, be absent, or incapacitated, or who may omit, decline, or from any cause cease to act as such Arbitrator, His Majesty the King of Sweden and Norway shall be requested to name one or more persons, as the case may be, to act as such Arbitrator or Arbitrators.

Article II.

The Arbitrators shall meet at Geneva, in Switzerland, at the earliest convenient day after they shall have been named, and shall proceed impartially and carefully to examine and decide all questions that shall be laid before them on the part of the Governments of the United States and Her Britannic Majesty respectively. All questions considered by the Tribunal, including the final award, shall be decided by a majority of all the Arbitrators.

Each of the High Contracting Parties shall also name one person to attend the Tribunal as its agent to represent it generally in all matters connected with the arbitration.

Article III.

The written or printed case of each of the two Parties, accompanied by the documents, the official correspondence, and other evidence on which each relies, shall be delivered in duplicate to each of the Arbitrators and to the agent of the other Party as soon as may be after the organization of the Tribunal, but within a period not exceeding six months from the date of the exchange of the ratifications of this Treaty.

Article IV.

Within four months after the delivery on both sides of the written or printed case, either Party may, in like manner, deliver in duplicate to each of the said Arbitrators, and to the agent of the other Party, a counter-case, and additional documents, correspondence, and evidence, in reply to the case, documents, correspondence, and evidence so presented by the other Party.

The Arbitrators may, however, extend the time for delivering such counter-case, documents, correspondence, and evidence, when, in their judgment, it becomes necessary, in consequence of the distance of the place from which the evidence to be presented is to be procured.

If in the case submitted to the Arbitrators either Party shall have specified or alluded to any report or document in its own exclusive possession without annexing a copy, such Party shall be bound, if the other Party thinks proper to apply for it, to furnish that Party with a copy thereof; and either Party may call upon the other, through the Arbitrators, to produce the originals or certified copies of any papers adduced as evidence, giving in each instance such reasonable notice as the Arbitrators may require.

Article V.

It shall be the duty of the agent of each Party, within two months after the expiration of the time limited for the delivery of the counter-case on both sides, to deliver in duplicate to each of the said Arbitrators and to the agent of the other party a written or printed argument showing the points and referring to the evidence upon which his Government relies; and the Arbitrators may, if they desire further elucidation with regard to any point, require a written or printed statement or argument, or oral argument by counsel upon it; but in such case the other Party shall be entitled to reply either orally or in writing, as the case may be.

Article VI.

In deciding the matters submitted to the Arbitrators, they shall be governed by the following three rules, which are agreed upon by the High Contracting Parties as rules to be taken as applicable to the case, and by such principles of International Law not inconsistent therewith as the Arbitrators shall determine to have been applicable to the case.

RULES.

A neutral Government is bound—

First, to use due diligence to prevent the fitting out, arming, or equipping, within its jurisdiction, of any vessel which it has reasonable ground to believe is intended to cruise or to carry on war against a Power with which it is at peace; and also to use like diligence to prevent the departure from its jurisdiction of any vessel intended to cruise or carry on war as above, such vessel having been specially adapted, in whole or in part, within such jurisdiction, to warlike use.

Secondly, not to permit or suffer either belligerent to make use of its ports or waters as the base of naval operations against the other, or for the purpose of the renewal or augmentation of military supplies or arms, or the recruitment of men.

Thirdly, to exercise due diligence in its own ports and waters, and, as to all persons within its jurisdiction, to prevent any violation of the foregoing obligations and duties.

Her Britannic Majesty has commanded her High Commissioners and Plenipotentiaries to declare that Her Majesty's Government can not assent to the foregoing rules as a statement of principles of International Law which were in force at the time when the claims mentioned in Article I. arose; but that Her Majesty's Government, in order to evince its desire of strengthening the friendly relations between the two countries and of making satisfactory provision for the future, agrees that, in deciding the questions between the two countries arising out of those claims, the Arbitrators should assume that Her Majesty's Government had undertaken to act upon the principles set forth in these rules.

And the High Contracting Parties agree to observe these rules as between themselves in future, and to bring them to the knowledge of other maritime Powers, and to invite them to accede to them.

Article VII.

The decision of the Tribunal shall, if possible, be made within three months from the close of the argument on both sides.

It shall be made in writing and dated, and shall be signed by the Arbitrators who may assent to it.

The said Tribunal shall first determine as to each vessel separately whether Great Britain has, by any act or omission, failed to fulfill any of the duties set forth in the foregoing three rules, or recognized by the principles of International Law not inconsistent with such rules, and shall certify such fact as to each of the said vessels. In case the Tribunal find that Great Britain has failed to fulfill any duty or duties as aforesaid, it may, if it think proper, proceed to award a sum in gross to be paid by Great Britain to the United States for all the claims referred to it; and in such case the gross sum so awarded shall be paid in coin by the Government of Great Britain to the Government of the United States, at Washington, within twelve months after the date of the award.

The award shall be in duplicate, one copy whereof shall be delivered to the agent of the United States for his Government, and the other copy shall be delivered to the agent of Great Britain for his Government.

Article VIII.

Each Government shall pay its own agent, and provide for the proper remuneration of the counsel employed by it and of the Arbitrator appointed by it, and for the expense of preparing and submitting its case to the Tribunal. All other expenses connected with the arbitration shall be defrayed by the two Governments in equal moieties.

Article IX.

The Arbitrators shall keep an accurate record of their proceedings, and may appoint and employ the necessary officers to assist them.

Article X.

In case the Tribunal finds that Great Britain has failed to fulfill any duty or duties as aforesaid, and does not award a sum in gross, the High Contracting Parties agree that a Board of Assessors shall be appointed to ascertain and determine what claims are valid, and what amount or amounts shall be paid by Great Britain to the United States on account of the liability arising from such failure, as to each vessel, according to the extent of such liability as decided by the Arbitrators.

The Board of Assessors shall be constituted as follows: One member thereof shall be named by the President of the United States, one member thereof shall be named by Her Britannic Majesty, and one member thereof shall be named by the Representative at Washington of His Majesty the King of Italy; and in case of a vacancy happening from any cause, it shall be filled in the same manner in which the original appointment was made.

As soon as possible after such nominations the Board of Assessors shall be organized in Washington, with power to hold their sittings there, or in New York, or in Boston. The members thereof shall severally subscribe a solemn declaration that they will impartially and carefully examine and decide, to the best of their judgment and according to justice and equity, all matters submitted to them, and shall forthwith proceed, under such rules and regulations as they may prescribe, to the investigation of the claims which shall be presented to them by the Government of the United States, and shall examine and decide upon them in such order and manner as they may think proper, but upon such evidence or information only as shall be furnished by or on behalf of the Governments of the United States and of Great Britain respectively. They shall be bound to hear on each separate claim, if required, one person on behalf of each Government, as counsel or agent. A majority of the Assessors in each case shall be sufficient for a decision.

The decision of the Assessors shall be given upon each claim in writing, and shall be signed by them respectively and dated.

Every claim shall be presented to the Assessors within six months from the day of their first meeting; but they may, for good cause shown, extend the time for the presentation of any claim to a further period not exceeding three months.

The Assessors shall report to each Government at or before the expiration of one year from the date of their first meeting the amount of claims decided by them up to the date of such report; if further claims then remain undecided, they shall make a further report at or before the expiration of two years from the date of such first meeting; and in case any claims remain undetermined at that time, they shall make a final report within a further period of six months.

The report or reports shall be made in duplicate, and one copy thereof shall be delivered to the Secretary of State of the United States, and one copy thereof to the Representative of Her Britannic Majesty at Washington.

All sums of money which may be awarded under this article shall be payable at Washington, in coin, within twelve months after the delivery of each report.

The Board of Assessors may employ such clerks as they shall think necessary.

The expenses of the Board of Assessors shall be borne equally by the two Governments, and paid from time to time, as may be found expedient, on the production of accounts certified by the Board. The remuneration of the Assessors shall also be paid by the two Governments in equal moieties in a similar manner.

Article XI.

The High Contracting Parties engage to consider the result of the proceedings of the Tribunal of Arbitration and of the Board of Assessors, should such

Board be appointed, as a full, perfect, and final settlement of all the claims hereinbefore referred to; and further engage that every such claim, whether the same may or may not have been presented to the notice of, made, preferred, or laid before the Tribunal or Board, shall, from and after the conclusion of the proceedings of the Tribunal or Board, be considered and treated as finally settled, barred, and thenceforth inadmissible.

ARTICLE XII.

The High Contracting Parties agree that all claims on the part of corporations, companies, or private individuals, citizens of the United States, upon the Government of Her Britannic Majesty, arising out of acts committed against the persons or property of citizens of the United States during the period between the thirteenth of April, eighteen hundred and sixty-one, and the ninth of April, eighteen hundred and sixty-five, inclusive, not being claims growing out of the acts of the vessels referred to in Article I. of this Treaty, and all claims, with the like exception, on the part of corporations, companies, or private individuals, subjects of Her Britannic Majesty, upon the Government of the United States, arising out of acts committed against the persons or property of subjects of Her Britannic Majesty during the same period, which may have been presented to either Government for its interposition with the other, and which yet remain unsettled, as well as any other such claims which may be presented within the time specified in Article XIV. of this Treaty, shall be referred to three Commissioners, to be appointed in the following manner, that is to say: One Commissioner shall be named by the President of the United States, one by Her Britannic Majesty, and a third by the President of the United States and Her Britannic Majesty conjointly; and in case the third Commissioner shall not have been so named within a period of three months from the date of the exchange of the ratifications of this Treaty, then the third Commissioner shall be named by the Representative at Washington of His Majesty the King of Spain. In case of the death, absence, or incapacity of any Commissioner, or in the event of any Commissioner omitting or ceasing to act, the vacancy shall be filled in the manner hereinbefore provided for making the original appointment; the period of three months in case of such substitution being calculated from the date of the happening of the vacancy.

The Commissioners so named shall meet at Washington at the earliest convenient period after they have been respectively named; and shall, before proceeding to any business, make and subscribe a solemn declaration that they will impartially and carefully examine and decide, to the best of their judgment, and according to justice and equity, all such claims as shall be laid before them on the part of the Governments of the United States and of Her Britannic Majesty, respectively; and such declaration shall be entered on the record of their proceedings.

Article XIII.

The Commissioners shall then forthwith proceed to the investigation of the claims which shall be presented to them. They shall investigate and decide such claims in such order and such manner as they may think proper, but upon such evidence or information only as shall be furnished by or on behalf of the respective Governments. They shall be bound to receive and consider all written documents or statements which may be presented to them by or on behalf of the respective Governments in support of, or in answer to, any claim, and to hear, if required, one person on each side, on behalf of each Government, as counsel or agent for such Government, on each and every separate claim. A majority of the Commissioners shall be sufficient for an award in each case. The award shall be given upon each claim in writing, and shall be signed by the Commissioners assenting to it. It shall be competent for each Government to name one person to attend the Commissioners as its agent, to present and support claims on its behalf, and to answer claims made upon it, and to represent it generally in all matters connected with the investigation and decision thereof.

The High Contracting Parties hereby engage to consider the decision of the Commissioners as absolutely final and conclusive upon each claim decided upon by them, and to give full effect to such decisions without any objection, evasion, or delay whatsoever.

Article XIV.

Every claim shall be presented to the Commissioners within six months from the day of their first meeting, unless in any case where reasons for delay shall be established to the satisfaction of the Commissioners, and then, and in any such case, the period for presenting the claim may be extended by them to any time not exceeding three months longer.

The Commissioners shall be bound to examine and decide upon every claim within two years from the day of their first meeting. It shall be competent for the Commissioners to decide in each case whether any claim has or has not been duly made, preferred, and laid before them, either wholly or to any and what extent, according to the true intent and meaning of this Treaty.

Article XV.

All sums of money which may be awarded by the Commissioners on account of any claim shall be paid by the one Government to the other, as the case may be, within twelve months after the date of the final award, without interest, and without any deduction save as specified in Article XVI. of this Treaty.

Article XVI.

The Commissioners shall keep an accurate record and correct minutes or notes of all their proceedings, with the dates thereof, and may appoint and employ a secretary, and any other necessary officer or officers, to assist them in the transaction of the business which may come before them.

Each Government shall pay its own Commissioner and agent or counsel. All other expenses shall be defrayed by the two Governments in equal moieties.

The whole expenses of the Commission, including contingent expenses, shall be defrayed by a ratable deduction on the amount of the sums awarded by the Commissioners, provided always that such deduction shall not exceed the rate of five per cent. on the sums so awarded.

Article XVII.

The High Contracting Parties engage to consider the result of the proceedings of this Commission as a full, perfect, and final settlement of all such claims as are mentioned in Article XII. of this Treaty upon either Government; and further engage that every such claim, whether or not the same may have been presented to the notice of, made, preferred, or laid before the said Commission, shall, from and after the conclusion of the proceedings of the said Commission, be considered and treated as finally settled, barred, and thenceforth inadmissible.

Article XVIII.

It is agreed by the High Contracting Parties that, in addition to the liberty secured to the United States fishermen by the Convention between the United States and Great Britain, signed at London on the 20th day of October, 1818, of taking, curing, and drying fish on certain coasts of the British North American Colonies therein defined, the inhabitants of the United States shall have, in common with the subjects of Her Britannic Majesty, the liberty, for the term of years mentioned in Article XXXIII. of this Treaty, to take fish of every kind, except shell-fish, on the sea-coasts and shores, and in the bays, harbors, and creeks, of the Provinces of Quebec, Nova Scotia, and New Brunswick, and the Colony of Prince Edward's Island, and of the several islands thereunto adjacent, without being restricted to any distance from the shore, with permission to land upon the said coasts and shores and islands, and also upon the Magdalen Islands, for the purpose of drying their nets and curing their fish; provided that, in so doing, they do not interfere with the rights of private property, or with British fishermen in the peaceable use of any part of the said coasts in their occupancy for the same purpose.

It is understood that the above-mentioned liberty applies solely to the sea fishery, and that the salmon and shad fisheries, and all other fisheries in rivers and the mouths of rivers, are hereby reserved exclusively for British fishermen.

Article XIX.

It is agreed by the High Contracting Parties that British subjects shall have, in common with the citizens of the United States, the liberty, for the term of

APPENDIX.

years mentioned in Article XXXIII. of this Treaty, to take fish of every kind, except shell-fish, on the eastern sea-coasts and shores of the United States north of the thirty-ninth parallel of north latitude, and on the shores of the several islands thereunto adjacent, and in the bays, harbors, and creeks of the said sea-coasts and shores of the United States and of the said islands, without being restricted to any distance from the shore, with permission to land upon the said coasts of the United States and of the islands aforesaid, for the purpose of drying their nets and curing their fish ; provided that, in so doing, they do not interfere with the rights of private property, or with the fishermen of the United States in the peaceable use of any part of the said coasts in their occupancy for the same purpose.

It is understood that the above-mentioned liberty applies solely to the sea fishery, and that salmon and shad fisheries, and all other fisheries in rivers and mouths of rivers, are hereby reserved exclusively for fishermen of the United States.

Article XX.

It is agreed that the places designated by the Commissioners appointed under the First Article of the Treaty between the United States and Great Britain, concluded at Washington on the 5th of June, 1854, upon the coasts of Her Britannic Majesty's Dominions and the United States, as places reserved from the common right of fishing under that Treaty, shall be regarded as in like manner reserved from the common right of fishing under the preceding articles. In case any question should arise between the Governments of the United States and of Her Britannic Majesty as to the common right of fishing in places not thus designated as reserved, it is agreed that a Commission shall be appointed to designate such places, and shall be constituted in the same manner, and have the same powers, duties, and authority as the Commission appointed under the said First Article of the Treaty of the 5th of June, 1854.

Article XXI.

It is agreed that, for the term of years mentioned in Article XXXIII. of this Treaty, fish-oil and fish of all kinds [except fish of the inland lakes, and of the rivers falling into them, and except fish preserved in oil], being the produce of the fisheries of the United States, or of the Dominion of Canada, or of Prince Edward's Island, shall be admitted into each country, respectively, free of duty.

Article XXII.

Inasmuch as it is asserted by the Government of Her Britannic Majesty that the privileges accorded to the citizens of the United States under Article XVIII. of this Treaty are of greater value than those accorded by Articles XIX. and XXI. of this Treaty to the subjects of Her Britannic Majesty, and this assertion is not admitted by the Government of the United States, it is further agreed that Commissioners shall be appointed to determine, having regard to the privileges accorded by the United States to the subjects of Her Britannic Majesty, as stated in Articles XIX. and XXI. of this Treaty, the amount of any compensation which, in their opinion, ought to be paid by the Government of the United States to the Government of Her Britannic Majesty in return for the privileges accorded to the citizens of the United States under Article XVIII. of this Treaty; and that any sum of money which the said Commissioners may so award shall be paid by the United States Government, in a gross sum, within twelve months after such award shall have been given.

Article XXIII.

The Commissioners referred to in the preceding article shall be appointed in the following manner, that is to say : One Commissioner shall be named by the President of the United States, one by Her Britannic Majesty, and a third by the President of the United States and Her Britannic Majesty conjointly; and in case the third Commissioner shall not have been so named within a period of three months from the date when this article shall take effect, then the third Commissioner shall be named by the Representative at London of His Majesty the Emperor of Austria and King of Hungary. In case of the death, absence, or incapacity of any Commissioner, or in the event of any Commissioner omitting or ceasing to act, the vacancy shall be filled in the manner hereinbefore provided for making the original appointment, the period of three months in case of such substitution being calculated from the date of the happening of the vacancy.

The Commissioners so named shall meet in the City of Halifax, in the Province of Nova Scotia, at the earliest convenient period after they have been respectively named, and shall, before proceeding to any business, make and subscribe a solemn declaration that they will impartially and carefully examine and decide the matters referred to them to the best of their judgment, and according to justice and equity; and such declaration shall be entered on the record of their proceedings.

Each of the High Contracting Parties shall also name one person to attend the Commission as its agent, to represent it generally in all matters connected with the Commission.

Article XXIV.

The proceedings shall be conducted in such order as the Commissioners appointed under Articles XXII. and XXIII. of this Treaty shall determine. They shall be bound to receive such oral or written testimony as either Government may present. If either Party shall offer oral testimony, the other Party shall have the right of cross-examination, under such rules as the Commissioners shall prescribe.

If in the case submitted to the Commissioners either Party shall have specified or alluded to any report or document in its own exclusive possession, without annexing a copy, such Party shall be bound, if the other Party thinks proper to apply for it, to furnish that Party with a copy thereof; and either Party may call upon the other, through the Commissioners, to produce the originals or certified copies of any papers adduced as evidence, giving in each instance such reasonable notice as the Commissioners may require.

The case on either side shall be closed within a period of six months from the date of the organization of the Commission, and the Commissioners shall be requested to give their award as soon as possible thereafter. The aforesaid period of six months may be extended for three months in case of a vacancy occurring among the Commissioners under the circumstances contemplated in Article XXIII. of this Treaty.

Article XXV.

The Commissioners shall keep an accurate record and correct minutes or notes of all their proceedings, with the dates thereof, and may appoint and employ a secretary, and any other necessary officer or officers, to assist them in the transaction of the business which may come before them.

Each of the High Contracting Parties shall pay its own Commissioner and agent or counsel; all other expenses shall be defrayed by the two Governments in equal moieties.

Article XXVI.

The navigation of the River St. Lawrence, ascending and descending, from the forty-fifth parallel of north latitude, where it ceases to form the boundary between the two countries, from, to, and into the sea, shall forever remain free and open for the purposes of commerce to the citizens of the United States, subject to any laws and regulations of Great Britain, or of the Dominion of Canada, not inconsistent with such privilege of free navigation.

The navigation of the Rivers Yukon, Porcupine, and Stikine, ascending and descending, from, to, and into the sea, shall forever remain free and open for the purposes of commerce to the subjects of Her Britannic Majesty and to the citizens of the United States, subject to any laws and regulations of either country within its own territory not inconsistent with such privilege of free navigation.

Article XXVII.

The Government of Her Britannic Majesty engages to urge upon the Government of the Dominion of Canada to secure to the citizens of the United States the use of the Welland, St. Lawrence, and other canals in the Dominion on terms of equality with the inhabitants of the Dominion; and the Government of the United States engages that the subjects of Her Britannic Majesty shall enjoy the use of the St. Clair Flats' Canal on terms of equality with the inhabitants of the United States, and further engages to urge upon the State Governments to secure to the subjects of Her Britannic Majesty the use of the several State canals connected with the navigation of the lakes or rivers traversed by or contiguous to the boundary-line between the Possessions of the High Contracting Parties, on terms of equality with the inhabitants of the United States.

Article XXVIII.

The navigation of Lake Michigan shall also, for the term of years mentioned in Article XXXIII. of this Treaty, be free and open for the purposes of commerce to the subjects of Her Britannic Majesty, subject to any laws and regulations of the United States or of the States bordering thereon not inconsistent with such privilege of free navigation.

Article XXIX.

It is agreed that, for the term of years mentioned in Article XXXIII. of this Treaty, goods, wares, or merchandise arriving at the ports of New York, Boston, and Portland, and any other ports in the United States which have been or may, from time to time, be specially designated by the President of the United States, and destined for Her Britannic Majesty's Possessions in North America, may be entered at the proper custom-house and conveyed in transit, without the payment of duties, through the territory of the United States, under such rules, regulations, and conditions for the protection of the revenue as the Government of the United States may from time to time prescribe; and, under like rules, regulations, and conditions, goods, wares, or merchandise may be conveyed in transit, without the payment of duties, from such Possessions through the territory of the United States for export from the said ports of the United States.

It is further agreed that, for the like period, goods, wares, or merchandise arriving at any of the ports of Her Britannic Majesty's Possessions in North America, and destined for the United States, may be entered at the proper custom-house and conveyed in transit, without the payment of duties, through the said Possessions, under such rules and regulations and conditions for the protection of the revenue as the Governments of the said Possessions may from time to time prescribe; and, under like rules, regulations, and conditions, goods wares, or merchandise may be conveyed in transit, without payment of duties, from the United States through the said Possessions to other places in the United States, or for export from ports in the said Possessions.

Article XXX.

It is agreed that, for the term of years mentioned in Article XXXIII. of this Treaty, subjects of Her Britannic Majesty may carry in British vessels, without payment of duty, goods, wares, or merchandise from one port or place within the territory of the United States upon the St. Lawrence, the Great Lakes, and the rivers connecting the same, to another port or place within the territory of the United States as aforesaid: Provided, that a portion of such transportation is made through the Dominion of Canada by land carriage and in bond, under such rules and regulations as may be agreed upon between the Government of Her Britannic Majesty and the Government of the United States.

Citizens of the United States may for the like period carry in United States vessels, without payment of duty, goods, wares, or merchandise from one port or place within the Possessions of Her Britannic Majesty in North America to another port or place within the said Possessions: Provided, that a portion of such transportation is made through the territory of the United States by land carriage and in bond, under such rules and regulations as may be agreed upon between the Government of the United States and the Government of Her Britannic Majesty.

The Government of the United States further engages not to impose any export duties on goods, wares, or merchandise carried under this article through the territory of the United States; and Her Majesty's Government engages to urge the Parliament of the Dominion of Canada and the Legislatures of the other Colonies not to impose any export duties on goods, wares, or merchandise carried under this article; and the Government of the United States may, in case such export duties are imposed by the Dominion of Canada, suspend, during the period that such duties are imposed, the right of carrying granted under this article in favor of the subjects of Her Britannic Majesty.

The Government of the United States may suspend the right of carrying granted in favor of the subjects of Her Britannic Majesty under this article, in case the Dominion of Canada should at any time deprive the citizens of the United States of the use of the canals in the said Dominion on terms of equality with the inhabitants of the Dominion, as provided in Article XXVII.

Article XXXI.

The Government of Her Britannic Majesty further engages to urge upon the Parliament of the Dominion of Canada and the Legislature of New Brunswick that no export duty, or other duty, shall be levied on lumber or timber of any kind cut on that portion of the American territory in the State of Maine watered by the River St. John and its tributaries, and floated down that river to the sea, when the same is shipped to the United States from the Province of New Brunswick. And, in case any such export or other duty continues to be levied after the expiration of one year from the date of the exchange of the ratifications of this Treaty, it is agreed that the Government of the United States may suspend the right of carrying hereinbefore granted under Article XXX. of this Treaty for such period as such export or other duty may be levied.

Article XXXII.

It is further agreed that the provisions and stipulations of Articles XVIII. to XXV. of this Treaty, inclusive, shall extend to the Colony of Newfoundland so far as they are applicable. But if the Imperial Parliament, the Legislature of Newfoundland, or the Congress of the United States, shall not embrace the Colony of Newfoundland in their laws enacted for carrying the foregoing articles into effect, then this article shall be of no effect; but the omission to make provision by law to give it effect, by either of the legislative bodies aforesaid, shall not in any way impair any other articles of this Treaty.

Article XXXIII.

The foregoing Articles XVIII. to XXV., inclusive, and Article XXX. of this Treaty, shall take effect as soon as the laws required to carry them into operation shall have been passed by the Imperial Parliament of Great Britain, by the Parliament of Canada, and by the Legislature of Prince Edward's Island on the one hand, and by the Congress of the United States on the other. Such assent having been given, the said articles shall remain in force for the period of ten years from the date at which they may come into operation; and further until the expiration of two years after either of the High Contracting Parties shall have given notice to the other of its wish to terminate the same; each of the High Contracting Parties being at liberty to give such notice to the other at the end of the said period of ten years or at any time afterward.

Article XXXIV.

Whereas it was stipulated by Article I. of the Treaty concluded at Washington on the 15th of June, 1846, between the United States and Her Britannic Majesty, that the line of boundary between the territories of the United States and those of Her Britannic Majesty, from the point on the forty-ninth parallel of north latitude up to which it had already been ascertained, should be continued westward along the said parallel of north latitude "to the middle of the channel which separates the continent from Vancouver's Island, and thence southerly, through the middle of the said channel and of Fuca Straits, to the Pacific Ocean;" and whereas the Commissioners appointed by the two High Contracting Parties to determine that portion of the boundary which runs southerly through the middle of the channel aforesaid were unable to agree upon the same; and whereas the Government of Her Britannic Majesty claims that such boundary-line should, under the terms of the Treaty above recited, be run through the Rosario Straits, and the Government of the United States claims that it should be run through the Canal de Haro, it is agreed that the respective claims of the Government of the United States and of the Government of Her Britannic Majesty shall be submitted to the arbitration and award of His Majesty the Emperor of Germany, who, having regard to the abovementioned article of the said Treaty, shall decide thereupon, finally and without appeal, which of those claims is most in accordance with the true interpretation of the Treaty of June 15, 1846.

Article XXXV.

The award of His Majesty the Emperor of Germany shall be considered as absolutely final and conclusive; and full effect shall be given to such award without any objection, evasion, or delay whatsoever. Such decision shall be given in writing and dated; it shall be in whatsoever form His Majesty may choose to adopt; it shall be delivered to the Representatives or other public Agents of the United States and of Great Britain, respectively, who may be actually at Berlin, and shall be considered as operative from the day of the date of the delivery thereof.

Article XXXVI.

The written or printed case of each of the two Parties, accompanied by the evidence offered in support of the same, shall be laid before His Majesty the Emperor of Germany within six months from the date of the exchange of the ratifications of this Treaty, and a copy of such case and evidence shall be communicated by each Party to the other, through their respective Representatives at Berlin.

The High Contracting Parties may include in the evidence to be considered by the Arbitrator such documents, official correspondence, and other official or public statements bearing on the subject of the reference as they may consider necessary to the support of their respective cases.

After the written or printed case shall have been communicated by each Party to the other, each Party shall have the power of drawing up and laying before the Arbitrator a second and definitive statement, if it think fit to do so, in reply to the case of the other party so communicated, which definitive statement shall be so laid before the Arbitrator, and also be mutually communicated in the same manner as aforesaid, by each Party to the other, within six months from the date of laying the first statement of the case before the Arbitrator.

Article XXXVII.

If, in the case submitted to the Arbitrator, either Party shall specify or allude to any report or document in its own exclusive possession without annexing a copy, such Party shall be bound, if the other Party thinks proper to apply for it, to furnish that Party with a copy thereof, and either Party may call upon the other, through the Arbitrator, to produce the originals or certified copies of any papers adduced as evidence, giving in each instance such reasonable notice as the Arbitrator may require. And if the Arbitrator should desire further elucidation or evidence with regard to any point contained in the statements laid before him, he shall be at liberty to require it from either Party, and he shall be at liberty to hear one counsel or agent for each Party, in relation to any matter, and at such time, and in such manner, as he may think fit.

Article XXXVIII.

The Representatives or other public Agents of the United States and of Great Britain at Berlin, respectively, shall be considered as the Agents of their respective Governments to conduct their cases before the Arbitrator, who shall be requested to address all his communications, and give all his notices, to such Representatives or other public Agents, who shall represent their respective Governments generally in all matters connected with the arbitration.

Article XXXIX.

It shall be competent to the Arbitrator to proceed in the said arbitration, and all matters relating thereto, as and when he shall see fit, either in person, or by a person or persons named by him for that purpose, either in the presence or absence of either or both Agents, and either orally or by written discussion or otherwise.

Article XL.

The Arbitrator may, if he think fit, appoint a secretary or clerk for the purposes of the proposed arbitration, at such rate of remuneration as he shall think proper. This, and all other expenses of and connected with the said arbitration, shall be provided for as hereinafter stipulated.

Article XLI.

The Arbitrator shall be requested to deliver, together with his award, an account of all the costs and expenses which he may have been put to in relation to this matter, which shall forthwith be repaid by the two Governments in equal moieties.

Article XLII.

The Arbitrator shall be requested to give his award in writing as early as convenient after the whole case on each side shall have been laid before him, and to deliver one copy thereof to each of the said agents.

Article XLIII.

The present Treaty shall be duly ratified by the President of the United States of America, by and with the advice and consent of the Senate thereof, and by Her Britannic Majesty; and the ratifications shall be exchanged either at Washington or at London within six months from the date hereof, or earlier if possible.

In faith whereof, we, the respective Plenipotentiaries, have signed this Treaty and have hereunto affixed our seals.

Done in duplicate at Washington the eighth day of May, in the year of our Lord one thousand eight hundred and seventy-one.

[L. S.]	HAMILTON FISH.
[L. S.]	ROBT. C. SCHENCK.
[L. S.]	SAMUEL NELSON.
[L. S.]	EBENEZER ROCKWOOD HOAR.
[L. S.]	GEO. H. WILLIAMS.
[L. S.]	DE GREY & RIPON.
[L. S.]	STAFFORD H. NORTHCOTE.
[L. S.]	EDWD. THORNTON.
[L. S.]	JOHN A. MACDONALD.
[L. S.]	MOUNTAGUE BERNARD.

And whereas the said Treaty has been duly ratified on both parts, and the respective ratifications of the same were exchanged in the city of London, on the seventeenth day of June, 1871, by Robert C. Schenck, Envoy Extraordinary and Minister Plenipotentiary of the United States, and Earl Granville, Her Majesty's Principal Secretary of State for Foreign Affairs, on the part of their respective Governments:

Now, therefore, be it known that I, ULYSSES S. GRANT, President of the United States of America, have caused the said Treaty to be made public, to the end that the same, and every clause and article thereof, may be observed and fulfilled with good faith by the United States and the citizens thereof.

In witness whereof, I have hereunto set my hand and caused the seal of the United States to be affixed.

Done at the City of Washington this fourth day of July, in the year of our [SEAL.] Lord one thousand eight hundred and seventy-one, and of the Independence of the United States the ninety-sixth.

U. S. GRANT.

By the President:
    HAMILTON FISH,
        Secretary of State.

DECISION AND AWARD

Made by the Tribunal of Arbitration constituted by virtue of the first Article of the Treaty concluded at Washington the 8th of May, 1871, between Her Majesty the Queen of the United Kingdom of Great Britain and Ireland and the United States of America.

Her Britannic Majesty and the United States of America having agreed by Article I. of the Treaty concluded and signed at Washington the 8th of May, 1871, to refer all the claims "generically known as the *Alabama* Claims" to a Tribunal of Arbitration to be composed of five Arbitrators, named:

One by Her Britannic Majesty,
One by the President of the United States,
One by His Majesty the King of Italy,
One by the President of the Swiss Confederation,
One by His Majesty the Emperor of Brazil;
and

Her Britannic Majesty, the President of the United States, H. M. the King of Italy, the President of the Swiss Confederation, and H. M. the Emperor of Brazil, having respectively named their Arbitrators, to wit:

Her Britannic Majesty:
   Sir Alexander James Edmund Cockburn, Baronet, a Member of Her Majesty's Privy Council, Lord Chief Justice of England;
The President of the United States:
   Charles Francis Adams, Esquire;
His Majesty the King of Italy:
   His Excellency Count Frederic Sclopis of Salerano, a Knight of the Order of the Annunciata, Minister of State, Senator of the Kingdom of Italy;
The President of the Swiss Confederation:
   Mr. James Stæmpfli;
His Majesty the Emperor of Brazil:
   His Excellency Marcos Antonio d'Araujo, Viscount of Itajubá, a Grandee of the Empire of Brazil, Member of the Council of H. M. the Emperor of Brazil, and his Envoy Extraordinary and Minister Plenipotentiary in France;

And the five Arbitrators above named having assembled at Geneva, in Switzerland, in one of the Chambers of the Hôtel de Ville, on the 15th of December, 1871, in conformity with the terms of the Second Article of the Treaty of Washington of the 8th of May of that year, and having proceeded to the inspection and verification of their respective powers, which were found duly authenticated, the Tribunal of Arbitration was declared duly organized.

The Agents named by each of the High Contracting Parties, by virtue of the same Second Article, to wit:

For Her Britannic Majesty:

Charles Stuart Aubrey, Lord Tenterden, a Peer of the United Kingdom, Companion of the Most Honorable Order of the Bath, Assistant Under-Secretary of State for Foreign Affairs;

And for the United States of America:

John C. Bancroft Davis, Esquire;

whose powers were found likewise duly authenticated, then delivered to each of the Arbitrators the printed Case prepared by each of the two Parties, accompanied by the documents, the official correspondence, and other evidence on which each relied, in conformity with the terms of the Third Article of the said Treaty.

In virtue of the decision made by the Tribunal at its first session, the Counter-Case, and additional documents, correspondence, and evidence, referred to in Article IV. of the said Treaty, were delivered by the respective Agents of the two Parties to the Secretary of the Tribunal on the 15th of April, 1872, at the Chamber of Conference, at the Hôtel de Ville of Geneva.

The Tribunal, in accordance with the vote of adjournment passed at their second session, held on the 16th of December, 1871, reassembled at Geneva on the 15th of June, 1872; and the Agent of each of the Parties duly delivered to each of the Arbitrators and to the Agent of the other Party the printed Argument referred to in Article IV. of the said Treaty.

The Tribunal having since fully taken into their consideration the Treaty, and also the cases, counter-cases, documents, evidence, and arguments, and likewise all other communications made to them by the two Parties during the progress of their sittings, and having impartially examined the same,

Has arrived at the decision embodied in the present Award:

Whereas, having regard to the Sixth and Seventh Articles of the said Treaty, the Arbitrators are bound under the terms of the said Sixth Article, "in deciding the matters submitted to them, to be governed by the three Rules therein specified, and by such principles of International Law not inconsistent therewith as the Arbitrators shall determine to have been applicable to the case;"

And whereas the "due diligence" referred to in the first and third of the said Rules ought to be exercised by neutral Governments in exact proportion to the risks to which either of the belligerents may be exposed from a failure to fulfill the obligations of neutrality on their part;

And whereas the circumstances out of which the facts constituting the subject-matter of the present controversy arose were of a nature to call for the exercise on the part of Her Britannic Majesty's Government of all possible solicitude for the observance of the rights and the duties involved in the Proclamation of Neutrality issued by Her Majesty on the 13th day of May, 1861;

And whereas the effects of a violation of neutrality committed by means of the construction, equipment, and armament of a vessel are not done away with by any commission which the Government of the belligerent Power benefited by the violation of neutrality may afterward have granted to that vessel: and the ultimate step, by which the offense is completed, can not be admissible as a ground for the absolution of the offender; nor can the consummation of his fraud become the means of establishing his innocence;

And whereas the privilege of exterritoriality accorded to vessels of war has been admitted into the law of nations, not as an absolute right, but solely as a proceeding founded on the principle of courtesy and mutual deference between different nations, and therefore can never be appealed to for the protection of acts done in violation of neutrality;

And whereas the absence of a previous notice can not be regarded as a failure in any consideration required by the law of nations in those cases in which a vessel carries with it its own condemnation;

And whereas, in order to impart to any supplies of coal a character inconsistent with the second Rule, prohibiting the use of neutral ports or waters as a base of naval operations for a belligerent, it is necessary that the said supplies should be connected with special circumstances of time, of persons, or of place, which may combine to give them such character;

And whereas, with respect to the vessel called the *Alabama*, it clearly results from all the facts relative to the construction of the ship at first designated by the "No. 290" in the port of Liverpool, and its equipment and armament in the vicinity of Terceira, through the agency of the vessels called the *Agrippina* and the *Bahama* dispatched from Great Britain to that end, that the British Government failed to use due diligence in the performance of its neutral obligations; and especially that it omitted, notwithstanding the warnings and official representations made by the diplomatic agents of the United States during the construction of the said "No. 290," to take in due time any effective measures of prevention, and that those orders which it did give at last for the detention of the vessel were issued so late that their execution was not practicable;

And whereas, after the escape of that vessel, the measures taken for its pursuit and arrest were so imperfect as to lead to no result, and therefore can not be considered sufficient to release Great Britain from the responsibility already incurred;

And whereas, in despite of the violations of the neutrality of Great Britain committed by the "290," this same vessel, later known as the Confederate cruiser *Alabama*, was on several occasions freely admitted into the ports of Colonies of Great Britain, instead of being proceeded against as it ought to have been in any and every port within British jurisdiction in which it might have been found;

And whereas the Government of Her Britannic Majesty can not justify itself for a failure in due diligence on the plea of the insufficiency of the legal means of action which it possessed;

Four of the Arbitrators, for the reasons above assigned, and the fifth for reasons separately assigned by him, are of opinion,

That Great Britain has in this case failed, by omission, to fulfill the duties prescribed in the first and the third of the Rules established by the Sixth Article of the Treaty of Washington.

And whereas, with respect to the vessel called the *Florida*, it results from all the facts relative to the construction of the *Oreto* in the port of Liverpool and to its issue therefrom, which facts failed to induce the Authorities in Great Britain to resort to measures adequate to prevent the violation of the neutrality of that nation, notwithstanding the warnings and repeated representations of the Agents of the United States, that Her Majesty's Government has failed to use due diligence to fulfill the duties of neutrality;

And whereas it likewise results from all the facts relative to the stay of the *Oreto* at Nassau, to her issue from that port, to her enlistment of men, to her supplies, and to her armament with the co-operation of the British vessel *Prince Alfred* at Green Cay, that there was negligence on the part of the British Colonial Authorities;

And whereas, notwithstanding the violation of the neutrality of Great Britain committed by the *Oreto*, this same vessel, later known as the Confederate cruiser *Florida*, was nevertheless on several occasions freely admitted into the ports of British Colonies;

And whereas the judicial acquittal of the *Oreto* at Nassau can not relieve Great Britain from the responsibility incurred by her under the principles of International Law; nor can the fact of the entry of the *Florida* into the Confederate port of Mobile, and of its stay there during four months, extinguish the responsibility previously to that time incurred by Great Britain:

For these reasons,

The Tribunal, by a majority of four voices to one, is of opinion,

That Great Britain has in this case failed, by omission, to fulfill the duties prescribed in the first, in the second, and in the third of the Rules established by Article VI. of the Treaty of Washington.

And whereas, with respect to the vessel called the *Shenandoah*, it results from all the facts relative to the departure from London of the merchant vessel the *Sea King*, and to the transformation of that ship into a Confederate cruiser under the name of the *Shenandoah*, near the island of Madeira, that the Government of Her Britannic Majesty is not chargeable with any failure, down to that date, in the use of due diligence to fulfill the duties of neutrality;

But whereas it results from all the facts connected with the stay of the *Shenandoah* at Melbourne, and especially with the augmentation which the British Government itself admits to have been clandestinely effected of her force by the enlistment of men within that port, that there was negligence on the part of the Authorities at that place:

For these reasons,

The Tribunal is unanimously of opinion,

That Great Britain has not failed, by any act or omission, to fulfill any of the duties prescribed by the Rules of Article VI. in the Treaty of Washington, or by the principles of International Law not inconsistent therewith, in respect to the vessel called the *Shenandoah*, during the period of time anterior to her entry into the port of Melbourne.

And by a majority of three to two voices, the Tribunal declares that Great Britain has failed, by omission, to fulfill the duties prescribed by the second and third of the Rules aforesaid, in the case of this same vessel, from and after her entry into Hobson's Bay, and is therefore responsible for all acts committed by that vessel after her departure from Melbourne on the 18th day of February, 1865.

And so far as relates to the vessels called

The *Tuscaloosa*
(Tender to the *Alabama*),
The *Clarence*,
The *Tacony*, and
The *Archer*
(Tenders to the *Florida*),

The Tribunal is unanimously of opinion,

That such Tenders or auxiliary vessels, being properly regarded as accessories, must necessarily follow the lot of their Principals, and be submitted to the same decision which applies to them respectively.

And so far as relates to the vessel called the *Retribution*,

The Tribunal, by a majority of three to two voices, is of opinion,

That Great Britain has not failed, by any act or omission, to fulfill any of the duties prescribed by the three Rules of Article VI. in the Treaty of Washington, or by the principles of International Law not inconsistent therewith.

And so far as relates to the vessels called

The *Georgia*,
The *Sumter*,
The *Nashville*,
The *Tallahassee*, and
The *Chickamauga*, respectively,

The Tribunal is unanimously of opinion,

That Great Britain has not failed, by any act or omission, to fulfill any of the duties prescribed by the three Rules of Article VI. in the Treaty of Washington, or by the principles of International Law not inconsistent therewith.

And so far as relates to the vessels called

The *Sallie*,
The *Jefferson Davis*,
The *Music*,
The *Boston*, and
The *V. H. Joy*, respectively,

The Tribunal is unanimously of opinion,

That they ought to be excluded from consideration for want of evidence.

And whereas, so far as relates to the particulars of the indemnity claimed by the United States, the costs of pursuit of the Confederate cruisers are not, in the judgment of the Tribunal, properly distinguishable from the general expenses of the war carried on by the United States,

The Tribunal is therefore of opinion, by a majority of three to two voices,

That there is no ground for awarding to the United States any sum by way of indemnity under this head.

And whereas prospective earnings can not properly be made the subject of compensation, inasmuch as they depend in their nature upon future and uncertain contingencies,

The Tribunal is unanimously of opinion,

That there is no ground for awarding to the United States any sum by way of indemnity under this head.

And whereas, in order to arrive at an equitable compensation for the damages which have been sustained, it is necessary to set aside all double claims for the same losses, and all claims for "gross freights" so far as they exceed "net freights;"

And whereas it is just and reasonable to allow interest at a reasonable rate;

And whereas, in accordance with the spirit and the letter of the Treaty of Washington, it is preferable to adopt the form of adjudication of a sum in gross, rather than to refer the subject of compensation for further discussion and deliberation to a Board of Assessors, as provided by Article X. of the said Treaty:

The Tribunal, making use of the authority conferred upon it by Article VII. of the said Treaty, by a majority of four voices to one, awards to the United States the sum of fifteen millions five hundred thousand Dollars in gold as the indemnity to be paid by Great Britain to the United States for the satisfaction of all the claims referred to the consideration of the Tribunal, conformably to the provisions contained in Article VII. of the aforesaid Treaty.

And, in accordance with the terms of Article XI. of the said Treaty, the Tribunal declares that all the claims referred to in the Treaty as submitted to the Tribunal are hereby fully, perfectly, and finally settled.

Furthermore, it declares that each and every one of the said claims, whether the same may or may not have been presented to the notice of, made, preferred, or laid before the Tribunal, shall henceforth be considered and treated as finally settled, barred, and inadmissible.

In Testimony whereof this present Decision and Award has been made in duplicate, and signed by the Arbitrators who have given their assent thereto, the whole being in exact conformity with the provisions of Article VII. of the said Treaty of Washington.

Made and concluded at the Hôtel de Ville of Geneva, in Switzerland, the 14th day of the month of September, in the year of our Lord one thousand eight hundred and seventy-two.

(Signed)   C. F. ADAMS.
(Signed)   FREDERIC SCLOPIS.
(Signed)   STÆMPFLI.
(Signed)   Vicomte d'ITAJUBÁ.